ACEQUIAS OF ALBUQUERQUE

WALKING ANCIENT WATERWAYS

JOYCE SALISBURY AND KIM HAFERMALZ

Published by The History Press
An imprint of Arcadia Publishing
Charleston, SC
www.historypress.com

Drone image of Corrales Main Drain. *Courtesy of Bob Hansen.*
Spring at Guttierez-Hubbel House. *Courtesy of Patty Carman.*

First published 2025

Manufactured in the United States

ISBN 9781467158688

Library of Congress Control Number: 2025940398

Notice: The information in this book is true and complete to the best of our knowledge. It is offered without guarantee on the part of the authors or The History Press. The authors and The History Press disclaim all liability in connection with the use of this book.

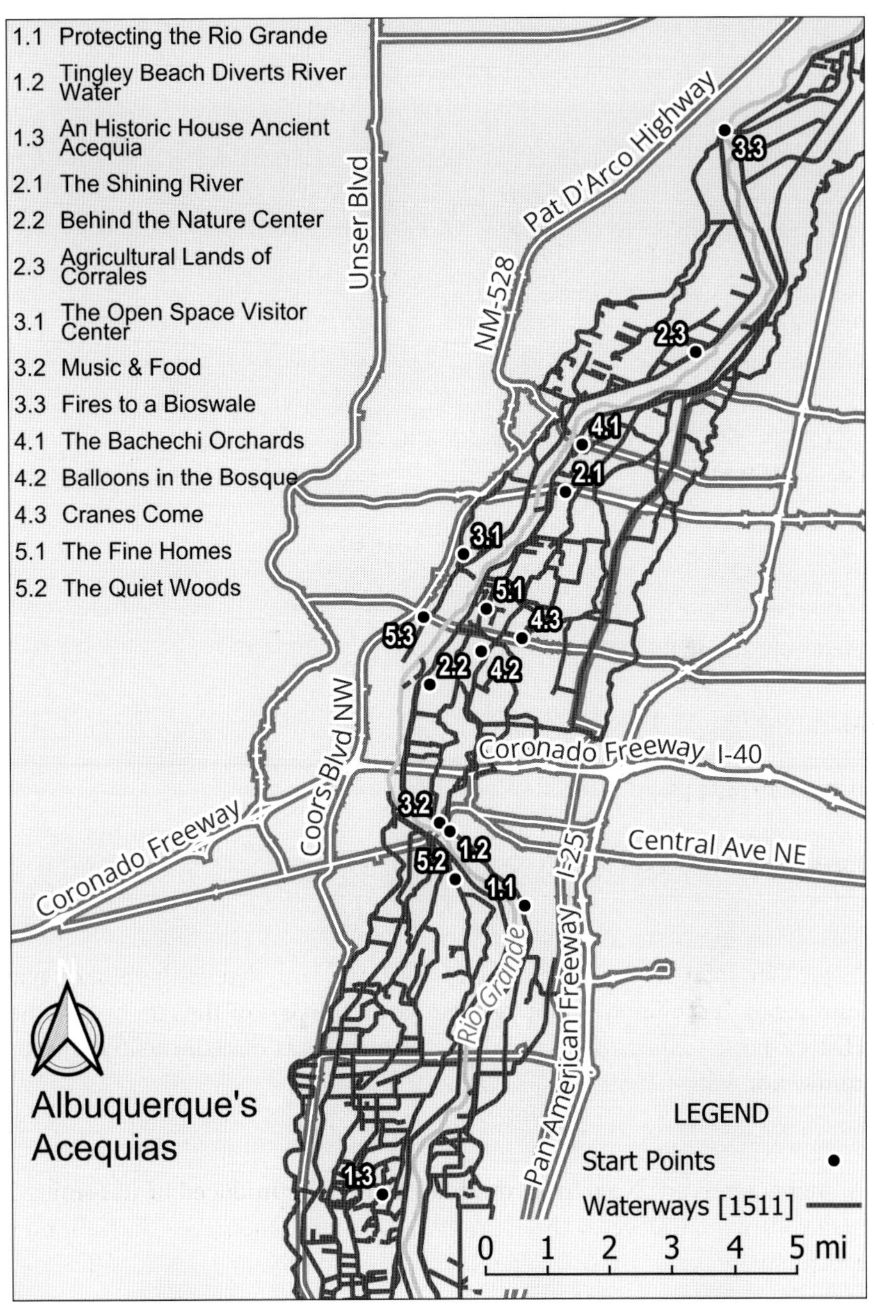

Albuquerque's acequias. *Roger Cardon.*

CONTENTS

Introduction

WATER CREATES COMMUNITIES

Albuquerque is located in the high desert, at about five thousand feet above sea level. There is an average of only nine inches of rainfall a year, and the air is so dry that what little moisture exists dries immediately. Here in the high desert, we expect to see dry desert plants and hearty heat-resistant animals, like rattlesnakes and lizards, and drought is a perennial problem. But Albuquerque has a special advantage: it lies in a valley with the Rio Grande River.

The city is located within a rift valley, that is a valley formed where the Earth's crust is thinning and pulling apart. It is flanked on the east by the Sandia Mountains and on the west by the volcanic landscape of the West Mesa. The Rio Grande winds through the city (and beyond) along its western edge. Unlike other great rivers, like the Colorado, the Rio Grande did not carve its path through the rock; instead, it followed the low land of the rift.

The Rio Grande flooded seasonally for millions of years. As the snow melted in the northern mountains, the rising water overflowed into the rift valley. Like the Nile and other flooding rivers, the Rio Grande left rich sediment within the valley. The river's water created a wide riparian (riverside) forest, as cottonwood trees evolved for millions of years alongside the floodplain of the river. This riparian forest is now called the Bosque (pronounced boh-skay), which is the Spanish word for "forest." This three-hundred-mile-long oasis of forest within this high desert extends from Santa Fe in the north to El Paso, Texas, in the south and is one of the largest cottonwood forests in the world.

This oasis is home to many forest animals and serves as a migratory route for many birds that came to count on this riparian forest long before humans arrived. But arrive we did. Some twelve thousand years ago Indigenous people settled in the area. Like everyone since, they needed the water to survive in this high desert.

As Indigenous farmers settled down, they quickly learned how to move the water from the shifting, flooding Rio Grande to irrigation ditches to water their fields. They planted the traditional "three sisters" crops—squash, beans and corn—that formed the basis for a healthy diet (and well-balanced fields). Here, during early agriculture, we see things that will shape the future of the region (and our walks). The Natives brought corn from Mexico to add to the native beans and squash. New plants and animals will repeatedly add layers to the Rio Grande valley.

In the late sixteenth century, Spanish explorers and colonists came north from Mexico to explore these unfamiliar lands along the Rio Grande. Finally, Juan de Oñate was given a contract for a permanent settlement, and he arrived in about 1598. He brought new animals—horses, sheep, cattle and dogs—and new plants into the valley.

The Spanish brought something else as well: a new way of cultivating in dry regions. In the high, dry plains of southern Spain, the Spanish built on the skills brought by the Muslims into Spain and dug gravity irrigation ditches. They added lateral ditches to existing rivers and diverted the water into the ditches that irrigated the lands. These ditches are called acequias (pronounced uh-*sey-ky*uhs).

These acequias have survived and been improved on for over four hundred years. The ditches follow the contours of the land and deliver water to fields and homes along the canals. As scholars of the acequias have described the intricate system, the acequias "have produced a greenbelt that extends the riparian zone, creating a microclimate oasis that sustains habitats." The water that is not used by the plants is returned through channels to be used downstream.[1]

New Mexico has over one thousand acequias irrigating over 160,000 acres of land. Albuquerque alone has hundreds. In 1986, the state passed a Water Resource Development Act that worked to protect the acequia system statewide.[2] Our map, called *Albuquerque's Acequias*, located next to the contents, was drawn from the Office of the State Engineer database for the Albuquerque area. It shows all the water conveyances in the area, including the acequias, canals, drains, etc. This map shows the astonishing network of waterways that weave through the city, and it demonstrates that the acequias

A license plate celebrating acequias. *Yahoo!News, www.news.yahoo.com.*

have shaped the development of the city itself, as residential homes nestle near the acequias that used to serve agricultural lands. The map shows the beginning point of our walks, and it shows that our fifteen walks only scratch the surface of this amazing network.

Not surprisingly, New Mexico residents recognize the importance of these ancient irrigation ditches that have become part of the life and geography of the city. In 2024, New Mexico made a new license plate available that celebrated the ancient acequias.

The phrase "acequias sangre viva" calls the acequias the "blood of life." This tagline was coined by Commissioner Mary Macareñas, and the commission said the phrase reflects the importance of these acequias that sustain the community.[3] Some of the proceeds from these plates will go to maintain and improve the community ditches.

There have always been more grassroots celebrations of the acequias. From the time of Spanish settlement, religious celebrations and processions have been linked to the cleaning of the ditches and the flow of the waters that bring the precious irrigation to the fields.[4] Here in Albuquerque, there is a more secular celebration in the form of the South Valley Acequia Run that takes place every April. People run alongside the ditches to raise awareness of the importance of the acequias and to raise money for sustainability efforts.[5] People here can't help but recognize the importance of water and the acequias that deliver it.

We will explore the features of these acequias in the course of this book, but there is one feature that shapes all our walks: the acequias are open-air ditches that require maintenance. They have to be cleaned out, and since they depend on gravity to move their water, the gates need to be opened and closed to control the water flow. This means that the land adjacent to the acequias has to be accessible. These are public domain paths that allow workers, walkers and bikers to use the ditches for labor and recreation. We can follow these irrigation ditches that serve as the lifeblood of our city.

As we walk the acequias, we not only note the rise and fall of the waters and the plants and animals that enjoy this urban oasis, but we also are reminded that the land remembers its history. We can trace the past in land use and the very creatures that live here. Thus, this book has become more than a book of walks; it joins history and the environment to tell the story of the growth and development of Albuquerque.

WALKING THE ACEQUIAS

Why walk? There has been a lot of research that shows walking is one of the best exercises for maintaining health, but new research has offered other reasons for us to enter the woods. Scientists have discovered stunning health improvements that come with time spent in green spaces like our Bosque. Research has measured results showing that spending two hours a week in the woods makes significant health improvements by all measures.[6] There are many books that explore this idea, and we particularly like Florence Williams's *The Nature Fix.*[7] So, for health and community, we are off on our walks.

Albuquerque is a city devoted to outdoor recreation. It has many parks and even more hiking and biking trails. The eastern mountains offer beautiful trails through the evergreen forests, and the western mesa lets hikers admire ancient petroglyphs and desert plants. However, this book focuses on walks that follow the water as it flows from the Rio Grande through neighborhoods and fields. This focus allows us to look closely at everything from forests and fields to large homes that depend on the water.

We have focused our walks in two counties: Bernalillo, which is where Albuquerque is located, and Sandoval County to the north of Bernalillo country. Sandoval is part of the growing Albuquerque region, but as we will see, it keeps its own character. The seals of both of these counties introduce some of the themes we will encounter during our walks.

The Bernalillo County seal has the Zia sun symbol on the top, which is a distinctive New Mexico emblem. It comes from the Zia Pueblo and signifies several things: the four seasons of the year; the four parts of the day, sunrise,

Top: Seal of Bernalillo County. *Bernalillo County, www.bernco.gov.*

Bottom: Seal of Sandoval County. *Sandoval County, www.sandovalcountynm.gov.*

noon, evening and night; and the four parts of life, childhood, youth, adulthood and old age. By including the Zia sun, Bernalillo County acknowledges its past and present indebtedness to the Indigenous people who first settled this land. The seal also has two mountain ranges, representing the Sandia and Manzano Ranges in the eastern part of the county. Finally, the seal shows eight sheep grazing in the valley. The sheep represent the eight land grants of the settlers, and they also recognize the contribution of the Spanish with their animal husbandry to the early life here.

The Sandoval County seal also recognizes the cultural layers that make up this region. It also features the Zia sun and the mountains that mark the valley. This seal includes the river, central to the valley's settlement. Furthermore, the seal also includes the moment when the Spanish settlers (with their covered wagon) met the Natives. This peaceful greeting wasn't the whole story, as you will see in the chapter "Walking to the Open Space Visitor Center," which features a walk where you can see the remnants of the interactions that brought violence to the valley.

Both seals reflect the importance of the layers of culture that mark the region. They also call attention to the movement of plants and animals into the area that has been so well served by the acequias. Finally, walkers will recognize these seals on the modern trucks that monitor the acequia ditches.

We want to emphasize that the walks we have chosen do not begin to explore the enriching Open Spaces of Albuquerque. We hope these walks will whet your appetite to explore further!

Beyond the geographic limit of this book, we have organized it in five sections, and each section contains three walks. We begin with a section called "Beginnings," which tells the history of controlling the Rio Grande to begin to move the waters into the acequias. In the land, we can trace the transformation of the river from a garbage dump to a shining beach of glass—and from a flooding river to a recreation area. Finally, in an ancient home, the remains of the oldest acequias appear to irrigate the fields.

The following four sections are organized by season. This emphasizes the shifting of both the waters and the growth they support. The acequias rise and fall as they irrigate the land and then recede for the winter. Of course, the plants, too, shift from early growth to full harvest, and birds migrate in different seasons. We invite readers to enjoy the walks at seasons different from the ones we have chosen; each season brings its own pleasures along the ditches.

HOW TO USE THIS BOOK

This guide isn't a standard walking handbook; it is a suggestion for walks. It will show what we saw as we went. We suggest you read each walk before you go to get an idea of what might be available. Then notice our maps for the walks, which will show you what paths we took. Each walk ranges between two and three miles long, but the lengths are optional. Most walks are out and back; you can go as far as you like. Do you want to walk farther? The acequias and Bosque paths offer lots of options for branching out, and there is always something interesting to see as you go. You might take a picture of our map to guide you on your way.

Through your walks, you can observe the kinds of things we saw. You will see a porcupine on a tree that was bare as we walked. Maybe you will see a beaver instead of the teeth marks and tracks that we saw. Each walk and each day are different.

As we walk through the Bosque, we become part of the acequia community, and in this introduction, we want to thank the community that helped create the book. A number of people contributed images that weave through these pages. Some photographers generously shared their photographs with us. The maps were drawn by Roger Cardon, who skillfully built our walks onto the base maps available on OpenStreetMap, which is licensed under the Open Data Commons Open Database License by the OpenStreetMap Foundation.[8] Jill Clark organized all the images and kept track of them so they could appear in the right places in this book. Finally, we thank the Mirehaven Walking Group, whose members formed a community of walkers as we all followed Kim as she led us through these wonderful acequias that continue to enrich the land we live in.

PART I

THE BEGINNINGS

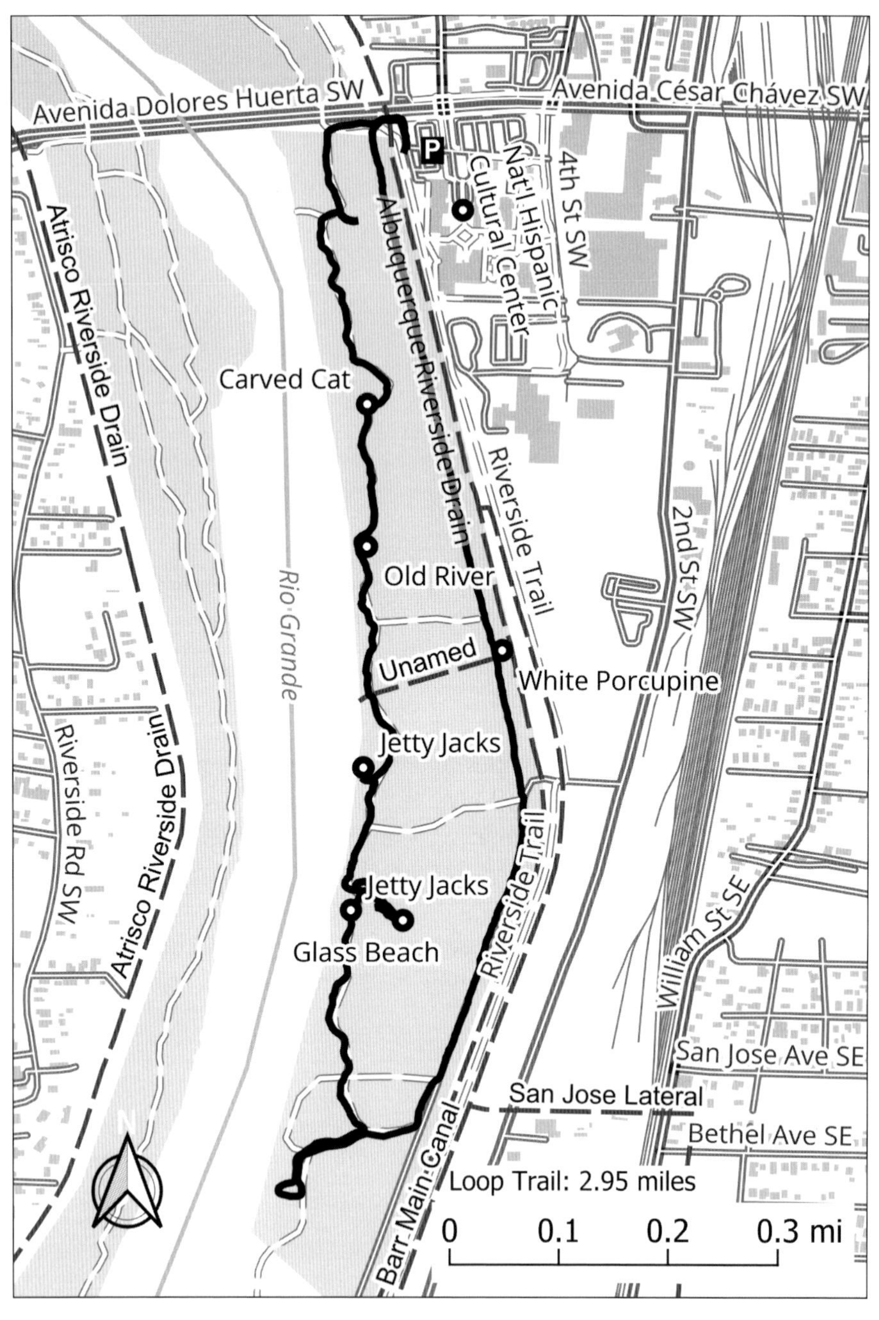

Roger Cardon.

1

PROTECTING THE RIO GRANDE

Today's walk in the south valley of Albuquerque shows some traces of the Rio Grande's history of development into a recreational and managed river system. All the water that flows into the acequias begins and ends here in the river, and these first few walks focus on the river, the source of all the abundance in this valley.

Rivers are the lifeblood of cities, but that doesn't mean we have always treated them well. People settled near rivers to facilitate transportation, to irrigate their fields and, unfortunately, to remove their garbage. People also use rivers as a source of recreation and food. Fishing, boating and swimming have always been draws for people. Of course, even a cursory reading of this list will show that many of these goals are incompatible. All cities across time have wrestled with the best use of their rivers, and this has been true of the cities along the Rio Grande.

In 1880, railways brought many settlers to the newly acquired territory of New Mexico. The federal government encouraged irrigation for new croplands, and the previous acequias were used and expanded. But there was no real plan, and the local acequia organizations that had been community-based didn't help with the many settlers who arrived and established farms along the riverbeds. But then disaster came.

Between 1897 and 1924, the middle Rio Grande valley experienced ten giant floods. Water flowed nearly thirty thousand cubic feet per second, flooding the land and wiping out entire villages.[9] It was clear that the river could not continue to exist in a floodplain and had to be managed.

Garbage was as much a problem as floods. With so much water, people assumed that any garbage dumped in the river would be washed away and become someone else's problem. (Though they probably didn't worry about downstream problems.) One famous environmentalist, Aldo Leopold, was appalled at the condition of the banks of the Rio Grande.

Aldo Leopold came to Albuquerque in 1915, starting his career with the newly formed U.S. Forest Service. He lived in Albuquerque for only five years, but his impact was tremendous. Among his concerns, he was horrified at the piles of garbage that lined the river. He wrote, "There are ten trainloads of tin cans there, not only on the city dump, but in and along the river itself."[10] He was among those who saw the potential of the river for recreation.

How best to tame both the river and the garbage? The growing population in Albuquerque and the increasingly complex nature of the water usage meant the state needed a centralized authority to manage all this. In 1925, the Middle Rio Grande Conservancy District, known as the MRGCD, was created. This agency is responsible for four counties and 150 miles of the Rio Grande River, and it manages the irrigation systems of the acequias and controls floods in the Albuquerque Basin. The MRGCD began to address the problems.

By 1935, the progress was stunning. The conservancy had built almost two hundred miles of levees along the riverbanks to stop the floods, essentially taming the Rio Grande and eliminating the adjacent floodplains. They built dams well to the north to store water and release it into irrigation canals for each section of the river. Hundreds of miles of ditches, laterals and canals were developed. This system continued to be improved over the years.

In the 1940s, the federal government authorized funds to continue to improve the Rio Grande. Jetty jacks were installed along the river to protect the levees and contain floods and the debris that floated down the river. These metallic structures still dot the Bosque. Cottonwoods were seeded along the banks to create this wonderful continuous cottonwood forest along the banks of the newly controlled river.

Once the river was controlled, laws were passed to stop the use of the river as a garbage dump. The conservancy district also began to implement Aldo Leopold's dream of having a riverside park that is protected for recreation.

With these thoughts in mind, let's begin our walk to see how much of this history we can still see imprinted on the land. We park our cars at the Hispanic Cultural Center, walk along the sidewalk and enter the Bosque on the trail.

The first thing we notice is that there has been extensive clearing of this wide floodplain next to the Rio Grande. The Forestry Division has designated this area as a wildfire mitigation area because it has had a number of forest fires in recent years. The mitigation involves clearing the dead trees and branches, and we can see piles of wood that have already been cleared.

Another aspect of protecting against wildfires involves clearing out some of the invasive plants that found their way here once the river's flood was controlled. The most invasive is the salt cedar, which uses a lot of water and burns very hot in fires. It won't be cleared entirely, but there is an ongoing effort to control its spread.

The cleared spaces let us admire the great cottonwood trees that were planted as part of the restoration plans for the riverbank. The seeded cottonwoods that were planted from the turn of the century to the 1940s have taken beautiful root. These Rio Grande cottonwoods have thick gray bark and triangular-shaped leaves. They can reach ninety feet in height, so they make a shady canopy in the summer. We walked here in late winter, so the bare branches offered us views of the river.

One of the wonderful features of walking in Albuquerque's Open Spaces is the presence of occasional public art. Every now and then, we came across a bit of art that blended with the landscape and brightened it up. As we wandered through the trees, I saw this lovely little carved cat made from an old stump. With coins as eyes, he watched us as we looked at him. What was the artist thinking? We don't know, but that's the nature of art, the viewer and observer bring their own experience. Some previous walker left the cat a candy, interacting with the hungry creature.

The river is wide here and shows the dynamic nature of its flow. Sandbars form as the river flows along, and in the spring, the cottonwoods will drop seeds. The seeds might land on the edge of the sand, quickly sprouting to form a new cottonwood grove along the moist, sunny banks. The trees will hold the banks and prevent erosion in a wonderful symbiotic relationship between the trees and the river.

The wide riverbank allows us to notice something else about the water usage in Albuquerque (and other riverbanks for that matter). As dramatic as the surface water is along the great river, equally important is the groundwater beneath, the aquifer that serves the city of Albuquerque. There are three water table monitors imbedded here, and my favorite is called "OldriverLF5."

Someone has decorated this post with the face of a woman in the cubist style, so she looks at us from all sides of the post. Periodically, water monitors

Don't
Crush the
Brush

Opposite: Interactive cat sculpture. *Courtesy of Jeri Burzin.*

Right: Cubist woman on Aquiver Tester. *Courtesy of Jeri Burzin.*

open the post and check the water table. The record of the water department shows that the water table for OldriverLF5 has consistently remained at about twenty-four feet below ground for the last few years. Is this enough? Development is drawing down the aquifer at a steady pace, and scientists are monitoring it regularly. As we walk, we remember that the water community includes the underground portion as well.

This thought brings another to mind as we walk by a cement-lined ditch that seems to be abandoned. During our forthcoming walks, we will see that some of the acequias have been lined with cement. This seemed like a good idea when we thought of water as simply a commodity that should be delivered most efficiently to its destination, perhaps to irrigate a field. But scientists discovered that this wasn't the best solution. Ancient dirt-lined acequias lost about 30 percent of their water to evaporation and seepage

Jetty Jacks in the Bosque. *Authors' collection.*

as the water flowed through the irrigation ditches, but this flow of water restored some of the water to the aquifer. Through these ancient acequias, the river supplied water to the groundwater. At various places in future walks, we will see some acequias that have left the cement lining broken in recognition that the aquifer is part of the water system.

While we notice the water, we also look up into the trees as we walk. The winter lets us spot another resident of the Bosque—porcupines. These North American porcupines are mostly nocturnal and browse in the cottonwood trees. They enjoy the leaves, buds, twigs and the bark. As we approached this black porcupine, I'm afraid we woke him up, and in his porcupine manner, he clacked his teeth loudly and hissed to warn us off. We took his picture and left him alone to enjoy the sunny branches by the river.

All these elements show us the success of the efforts of reclaiming the riverside as a recreational area. But there are also reminders of the river's past as it was slowly brought under control. We can see jetty jacks near the riverbank almost grown over with plants as they did their job of holding back the river floods. These were erected in the 1940s and 1950s, and as we continued our walk, we came across lines of jetty jacks that were rusted but intact. These rusting sixteen-foot-tall X-shaped forms march in a protective line across the old floodplain.

Beach of shimmering glass. *Authors' collection.*

In 2024, the New Mexico legislature set aside millions of dollars to remove the old jetty jacks as part of the restoration of the Bosque. The jacks are serious impediments to firefighters and are eyesores in the woods. We know their removal will be an improvement, but we will kind of miss the sharp contrast of the straight lines of the jacks with the curved organic lines of the forest. Historians and photographs will have to remember the important role of the jetty jacks in taming the river.

The jacks remind us that we are tracing the path back in time to when the Rio Grande wasn't the recreational area we enjoy today. We find a path that turns to the left as we move from the pristine Bosque back in time. We walk toward the old levee that was first built to hold back the river; we see the sun glisten on a beach of glass. The photo on page 21 shows this span of broken glass. The beauty of the colors of the glass and the designs visitors have made of the glass obscures the reality of the fact that this was a garbage dump through the 1940s.

The dump was periodically burned to remove organic, rotting material, but the broken glass survived the fires. Some wanderers through here find old bottles and broken crockery from old hotels. The cleanup of the riverbank that Aldo Leopold envisioned included moving the garbage dump from the river to landfills elsewhere, but as we so often see, the land remembers. And that's certainly true of this interesting glass beach.

We leave the glass beach and head back into the Bosque to walk a little farther south until we find a path around the glass that leads back east. Taking this path, we walk up to a levee, part of the original boundaries set up to protect Albuquerque from the floods of the Rio Grande. This is the same levee system that proved inadequate, requiring the jetty jacks to be erected. We walk along the levee, heading back north to the Hispanic Cultural Center.

On our right is the Albuquerque Riverside Drain that parallels the river and forms another piece of the flood control pattern. Farther north, Durán's acequia flows into this drain, bringing the water south and eventually back into the river. As we walk, we can see a flood control gate opening to release more water into the drain. We can't go far without being reminded of the constant efforts that go into using the water.

Before we reach the parking lot, we see one more fine glimpse of wildlife that shares the Bosque. Here by the levee in a budding cottonwood tree is a white porcupine. This one doesn't have to eat the bark; he can enjoy the fresh new leaves just coming out.

This is a perfect ending to our walk. In a short two miles, we have moved a couple of centuries in time. The Rio Grande has changed from a garbage dump to a carefully managed and protected river. It once more became a community of water that shelters cottonwoods, groundwater, humans, artists and hungry porcupines that enjoy the sunshine.

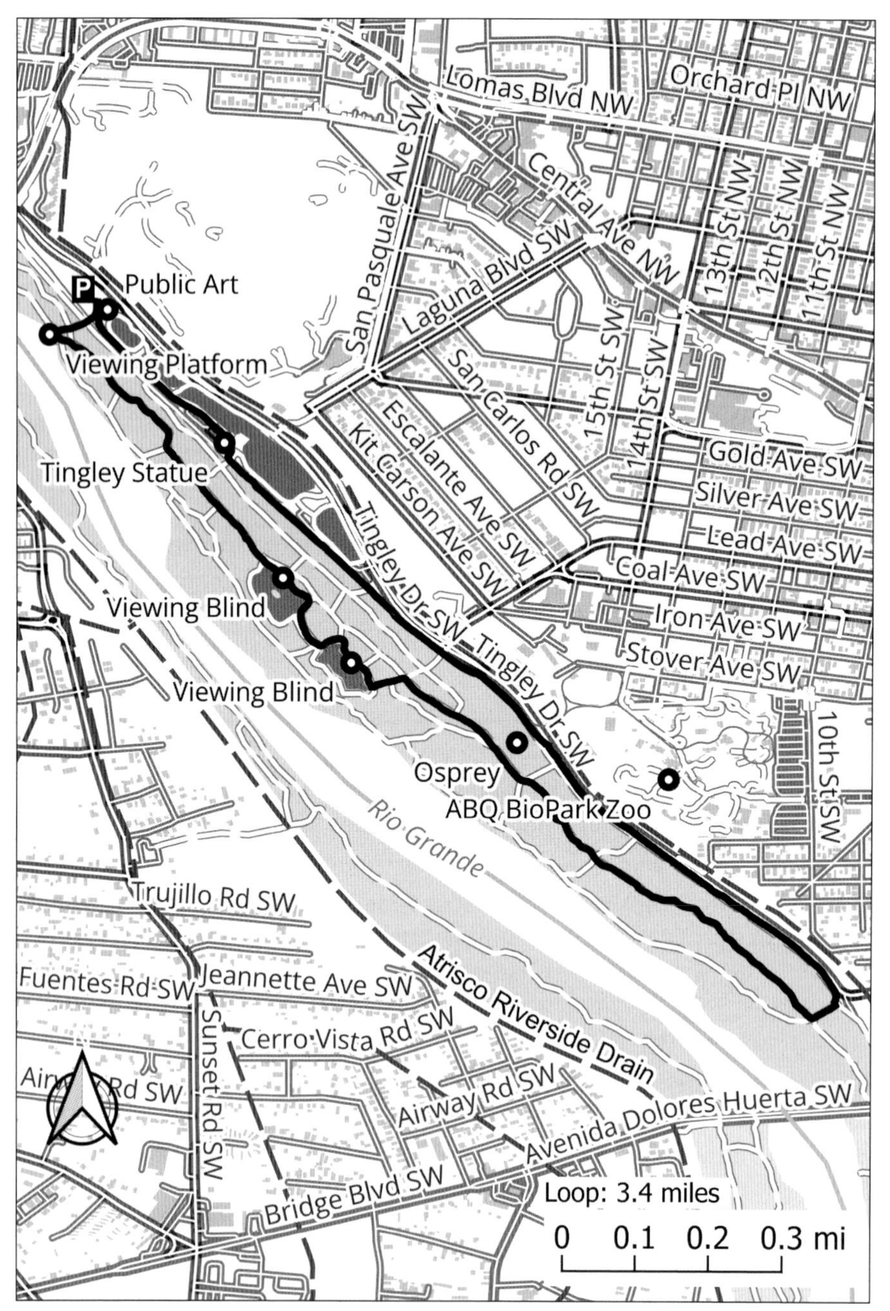

Roger Cardon.

2

RIO GRANDE AS RECREATION

In 1931, Clyde Tingley had an idea to turn the rushing Rio Grande into a gentle recreation area for the people of Albuquerque. He did so with energy and political connections, and during our walk, we will recognize, enjoy and celebrate his accomplishment.

Tingley served as city alderman beginning in 1916, which began his long political career that spanned forty years. He was governor of New Mexico for two terms beginning in 1934, and then he returned to Albuquerque to serve as city commissioner and local leader. He resigned from political life in 1955 and died in 1960. He served during the transformative years, when America was coming out of the Great Depression, and he had a close relationship with President Franklin Roosevelt. With his connections, Tingley brought federal money to Albuquerque through the Works Progress Administration (WPA). What to do with the money?

Tingley was obviously influenced by movements to turn the city into a recreational area. He knew of and shared Aldo Leopold's desire to turn the river from a dump to a protected area, and he had other ideas, too. Tingley funded a community center, a baseball stadium and other local projects. However, his most significant project was on the banks of the Rio Grande in the center of the city. He began this project in 1931.

We have seen how the glass beach was a remnant of the use of the river as a city dump, and there was another dump farther north along the Rio Grande, along Central Avenue. Tingley decided to eliminate this eyesore (and source of pollution) in a more dramatic way. Instead of burning the garbage and potentially creating another glass beach, he commissioned the newly formed Middle Rio Grande Conservancy District to dredge the dump. Great cranes were brought to the shore, trucks were loaded with the filth and tons of earth and debris were moved. They didn't level the land; they dug deep holes to prepare for the waters.

Then the water from the Rio Grande was diverted, and engineers created a series of ponds. This region was originally known as Conservancy Beach in recollection of the reclamation project. After World War II, the area was named Ernie Pyle Beach, after the famous war correspondent. Now, it is called Tingley Beach to remember the energy and contribution of its founder.

The engineers did more than create a diversionary canal to fill the ponds; they built a series of levees to prevent flooding, and in the process, the river itself moved to the west, leaving other ponds along the walking paths that are filled with wildlife. Indeed, these wetlands form a real conservancy area.

Tingley's ponds first served as popular swimming beaches. Photographs from the 1940s show many swimmers relaxing along the sandy levees in their swimsuits. The ponds were deep enough that they had high diving platforms. The city employed lifeguards to keep the throngs safe, but the lifeguards themselves caused a problem. A city commission report claimed the lifeguards were neglecting their duties and engaging in "too much talking to girls and public necking."[11] These halcyon days of sun, swimming and flirting came to an end in the 1950s with a terrible epidemic.

All over the country in the late 1940s and 1950s, the summers brought an upsurge of the dreaded disease polio. People died or were paralyzed. Parents kept their children away from public swimming pools, and many closed all over the country. The swimming beach at Tingley Beach was abandoned, and the lifeguards had to find other work.

Beginning in 2020, we learned how epidemics like COVID can change so many elements of life. The example of the polio epidemic shows that epidemics can change even the use and shape of the land. What to do with swimming ponds when no one is swimming? In 1954, Tingley Beach reopened, though as a fishing beach, where visitors could distance themselves from each other and the illnesses they feared. We'll look more closely at these ponds as we stroll by.

Let's start our walk. This walk is a two-mile loop that begins in the dirt parking lot slightly to the north of the beach. We walk west up the steps from the parking lot toward the river and then cross the bike path and enter the tree-covered Bosque. There are viewing platforms at the edge

Ducks in ponds at Tingly Beach. *Authors' collection.*

of the river, so we can watch the slow-moving waters. The river is shallow here, and we can see a black lab dog fetching a stick in the waters. We've never met a lab who didn't take advantage of each body of water to play, and this one is no different.

We walk south through the Bosque, seeing the familiar cottonwood trees and the scrub underbrush. This path leads to two ponds that were created when the Rio Grande shifted west. The first pond has a viewing blind that looks over the wonderful wetland that has been carved out of the shore. We are walking in early spring; the ducks are pairing up, and there are plenty of spaces along the shore for them to nest. In just over a month, we should see ducklings along this pond.

The Bosque offers shelter to many kinds of water birds. We see a flock of ring-necked ducks drifting along the water. Yes, that's what they are called, even though they don't have rings around their necks. They make a pleasant change from the more usual wood ducks that enjoy the ponds.

The viewing blind on the edge of the pond is there to let people watch the animals without scaring them off, but the animals are all used to being fed so they come close to the blind. Even turtles that are usually relaxing in the sun on a bank swim rapidly (for turtles) to see if we are offering them any food. With trial and error, we learn that the turtles like corn tortillas best.

These are western box turtles, common and native to this region. We also see a snapping turtle raise his serpentine head above the water with his beaked jaws open. He, too, is native but less readily observable. He's probably hoping for food that's more interesting than the bits of lettuce and tortilla that we feed the turtles.

The ponds have bridges that lead to side trails for exploration, but we continue south along the main trail, returning back into the Bosque. In the woods, we encounter some serious bird watchers. Armed with their binoculars and knowledge of the local birds, they tell us they have seen—and heard—western king birds and western bluebirds. We take their word for it and continue south.

Before long, we hear a loud cacophony of unrecognizable sounds. It turns out we have approached the ABQ BioPark Zoo. The monkeys are chattering and even barking loudly! They drown out any bird sounds in the woods, so we decide to turn left, going east to climb up a gentle slope. This was originally a levee used to hold back floodwaters. Now, it is a flat bike path, and we walk along it, heading back north.

As we walk by the back of the zoo, we can see elephants and hear the monkeys calling. In 2005, Tingley Beach became part of the ABQ BioPark that includes the zoo, an aquarium and a botanical garden. This combination increased the recreation and conservation value of this entire area along the river far beyond Tingley's initial vision for cleaning up the riverside dump. It has been a great success story.

The success has not been for humans alone, as the wildlife has also flourished. As we walk along, we are treated to a rare sight. An osprey lands on a high branch near us with a fish he has taken from the river. Sadly, he's

Turtles at viewing station at Tingly Beach. *Authors' collection.*

too high for our cameras to capture, but he's a wonderful sight. We can see ospreys in Albuquerque between March and May as they make their way north to nest. The Bosque is a wonderful corridor for migrating birds, and we are lucky to have seen this one.

As we continue north, the roof of the old Tingley Beach train station comes into view. This is now a stop for a shuttle that goes all the way to the zoo. There is a break in the fence, and we turn right to leave the levee bordering the Bosque and enter the space of Tingley Beach proper.

Right: Statue of Mayor Tingley. *Authors' collection.*

Below: Award-winning artwork at Tingley Beach. *Authors' collection.*

The front of the old train station is landscaped with beautiful flowers, and there is a statue of Mayor Tingley tipping his hat to visitors and extending his hand for a welcoming handshake. The bronze of his hand is shiny from generations of visitors shaking it. His wife, Carrie, is shown sitting on a bench greeting a child. This statue was installed here in 2000 to celebrate the couple's many contributions to the region.

Beyond the statue, we come to the ponds that were initially excavated so many years ago. Since the polio scare, the swimming beach is has disappeared, and the sand banks have been replaced by cement sidewalks and parking areas to accommodate visitors. But now, instead of swimming, families come to fish and picnic and enjoy the day.

There is one catch-and-release pond that is stocked with rainbow trout. More popular is the fishing pond. This one is restocked about once a month, so it is always full of fish. People catch trout, bass and catfish. We congratulated a young girl who was proudly displaying a string of five trout she caught that day.

As is pleasantly usual everywhere in Albuquerque, Tingley Beach has some interesting public art (beyond the statue of Mr. and Mrs. Tingley). The bottom photograph on page 98 shows a wonderful sculpture of a man catching a large gar. This sculpture was installed in 1997, and it was made by a famous metal sculptor, Joe Barrington. It perfectly celebrates the transformation of the beach to fishing ponds, though no one can catch a large gar like this one today.

Public art remains a central component to Albuquerque's open spaces. In 2007, more public art pieces were installed here as part of a public support of art program. Now visitors can enjoy sometimes-whimsical sculptures of boats, fish and birds to echo the natural wonders we've been enjoying. The bottom photograph on page 30 shows one of the prize-winning works that rise above the beach.

As we walk past the families enjoying the ponds, we have to dodge the many Canadian geese who spend their time here. As is the nature of geese, they are not afraid of us—not even of the dogs that walk along with us. They are shamelessly begging for food that they have become accustomed to, even as they stand under the "do not feed the geese" signs.

We reach our cars and leave this fine recreation area. As we enjoy this area, it is easy to forget that the waters of the Rio Grande are not just for pleasure. They have to go to work. Once the river was cleaned and controlled, the waters were needed for agriculture. It is time for us to walk and find the irrigation ditches—the acequias.

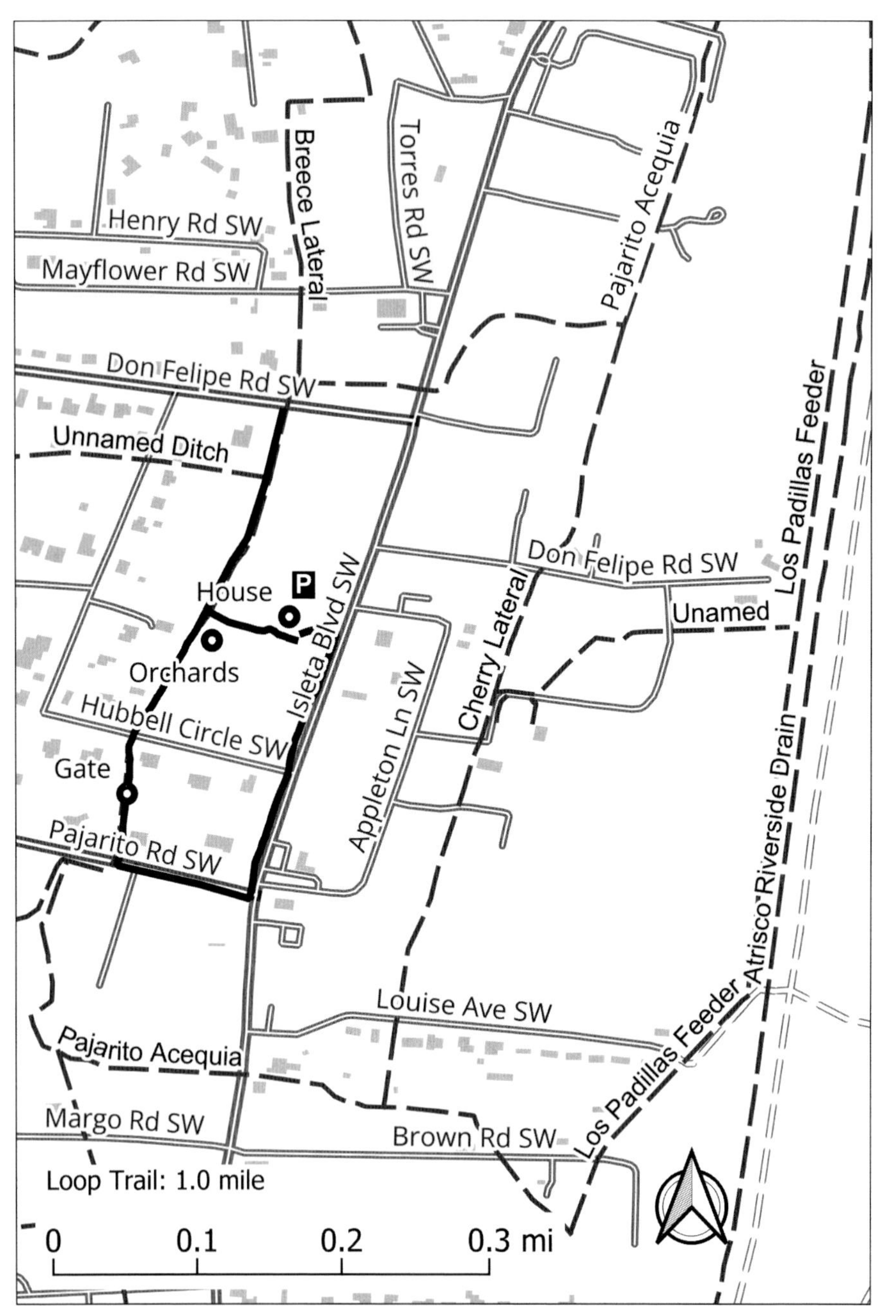

Roger Cardon.

3

A HISTORIC HOUSE AND ANCIENT ACEQUIA

In 1598, the Spanish explorer Don Juan de Oñate came to New Mexico north from Mexico City with five hundred settlers and soldiers and seven thousand animals, including cattle, sheep, horses and dogs. When the settlers arrived, they were immediately confronted with the problems of agriculture in the high desert. They observed the Indigenous tribes who channeled rainfall runoff and dug small irrigation ditches. In fact, the earliest Spanish laws claimed that if irrigation ditches were used by the Natives, no one could take them.[12] However, the Spanish wanted to irrigate larger swaths of land. To do that, they brought their expertise of what had worked in the dry southern lands of Spain, Andalucia and Valencia.

In southern Spain, people had a long tradition of irrigation and, perhaps more importantly, managing the use of the scarce water at a local level. The Tribunal de las Aguas, or Court of the Waters, is the world's oldest water court, founded in 960 CE, during the time of the Muslim caliphates of southern Spain. This court, which still meets at the front of the cathedral in Valencia, lets community members decide how to allocate the area's scarce water among them. This community control of water depended on a series of irrigation ditches, called acequias, and community investment in maintaining the ditches. This is what the Spanish settlers brought to New Mexico in the early seventeenth century.

The new settlers expanded on Native practices but tackled the great Rio Grande itself. They diverted waters, building dams made of logs, brush, rocks and anything else they could find. Then at the diversion dam, they dug the acequia madre, the mother ditch or main canal, to move the water to the fields. From the acequia madre, they dug lateral ditches cut perpendicular from the main canal to irrigate individual parcels of land. These laterals were called *sangrias*, which means "blood," reminding us that the water was the lifeblood of the community.

Finally, the water was guided to a drain channel, returning the water to the river. This whole acequia system was based on the idea that people were borrowing the water from the river, using it and returning it to its source. Water wasn't a commodity to own but part of the community of people, plants, animals and the river itself.

The earliest founding documents of New Mexico show the essential preoccupation with building and maintaining the acequias. A 1691 letter from Governor Diego de Vargas to the viceroy said that the kingdom of New Mexico was struggling with the flooding of the Rio Grande and needed dams and acequias to try to control the waters. As we have seen in the two previous chapters, controlling the great river would take a while. The Certificate of Founding of Albuquerque in 1706 confirmed the presence of irrigation ditches that helped create pasturage and fields.[13] Acequias were part of the very founding of New Mexico.

The early acequias were always controlled by the communities. The people who used the ditches cleaned them out every spring so the waters could flow. Just like in Spain, they decided how to allocate the water among them, and they designated a person to be in charge of opening the side ditches for the water to flow. This person was the *mayordomo*, who managed both the water system and the workers who maintained it. They helped make sure the water was equitably allocated. It was also the mayordomo's job to consider the weather and make decisions on how much water everyone would get. In times of plenty of water, the job was easy. In times of drought, the mayordomo had to make sure all the farmers suffered equally and equitably.

By the end of the eighteenth century, there were some 164 community ditches in New Mexico, and in the next century the numbers grew exponentially.[14] Figures compiled in 1936 show that there were 345 miles of drainage canals, 250 miles of main irrigation ditches (acequias madres) and nearly 400 miles of old lateral irrigation ditches (the local sangrias) in the middle Rio Grande valley alone. The federal government allocated money to rehabilitate these old constructions. The walks we take will allow us to explore some of these essential acequias that have made the settlement of New Mexico possible and prosperous.

Today, we will go to the Gutiérrez-Hubbell House in the South Valley of Albuquerque. The Gutiérrez-Hubbell House is located on Isleta Boulevard. Today, this road is unremarkable, but in the colonial period, the road was called El Camino Real de Tierra Adentro, the "Royal Road of the Interior." This was the earliest Euro-American trade route in the United States. It extended some 1,600 miles from Mexico City north of Santa Fe, and some of its earliest campsites and settlements became today's modern cities in the Rio Grande valley, a river the Spaniards called Rio del Norte, or "Northern River."

In the 1700s, a woman named Josefa Baca acquired a land grant of Pajarito along the Camino Real. This land had a large hacienda and extensive lands, where Josefa raised 950 head of sheep, horses, cattle and goats. The current neighborhood of the village of Pajarito grew up around this original hacienda. Josefa's son Antonio sold the tract of land to a relative, Clemente Gutiérrez. This land was originally a forty-thousand-acre estate. They willed the land to their great-granddaughter Julianita. Julianita married an easterner, James Hubbell, in 1849, and they had twelve children, creating a wealthy and influential dynasty in the area. Descendants of Julianita and James continued to live in the house until the 1990s, though the hacienda's acreage had been much reduced. In 2020, the property, now about ten acres, was bought by Bernalillo County, and it is now managed by the National Park Service.

We park the car adjacent to the plaza of the old house. This outdoor space had originally been surrounded by walls and was the heart of the life of the house. Children played, servants worked and the family relaxed in the shade of the porch that surrounded the old house.

We decide to tour the outdoor spaces before we enter the house. We walk west toward one of the oldest acequias in the region. This is the acequia madre, the mother ditch, of Pajarito, named after the region of the first land grant. Juan Gutiérrez had this ditch hand dug by his workers sometime around 1830. He used it to irrigate his orchards and gardens, and his fields prospered. He soon gave shares in this two-mile ditch to two neighboring landowners, and the three families maintained and worked it together for many years. Juan served as the mayordomo, regulating how much water each plot of land received in the manner of the old traditions in Spain. Juan died in 1875, but before he died, he gave ownership of the acequia to all the members of the Pajarito land grant. At that time, it became a community ditch, owned by the people. In the 1920s, its maintenance was turned over to the Middle Rio Grande Conservancy

District, which collects water fees and serves as mayordomo to determine how much water each property gets.

As we walk toward the acequia, we pass by the orchards and fields that have been irrigated by this acequia for over a century. The orchards have apple, cherry and peach trees and one amazingly ancient plum tree. Next to the orchards are gardens, which are now used as educational resources to teach people how to grow various foods.

We reach the two-mile-long branch of the Pajarito Acequia and turn north to walk along its banks. Before we started our walk, we looked at a map of the acequias in this area. Because it has been settled for such a long time, the network of ditches is impressive. The water enters the Cherry lateral from the Los Padillas Feeder farther north and then enters a network of ditches before it moves into the Los Padillas Acequia to the Atrisco Riverside Drain before returning back to the Rio Grande. As we walk this old ditch, we're reminded of how connected these communities are by the water.

Of course, as the water flows, we'd have no way of knowing how old the ditch is without the wonderful cottonwoods that line its banks. These centuries-old trees are amazing; their roots must go very deep to keep the old trees hanging precariously along the bank. In places, the trees grow above the ditch to join together, making a cooling canopy even in the hottest weather.

We reach Don Felipe Road, where the Pajarito Acequia curves off to the east, so we turn around and backtrack along the ditch the way we came. As we reach one of the gates that crosses the acequia, we meet a man standing on the edge of the gate, closing it with a wrench. We stop to talk. He's one of the property owners along here who has water rights. He is closing this check gate in order to raise the water level so he can open the turnout gate to release water into his land. He told us it is his turn to use the water; he is allocated a certain day and a certain number of hours. We asked him what happens if he exceeds his allotment, and he told us that the "ditch rider" sent by the Middle Rio Grande Conservancy District would put a lock on his turnout gate so he could no longer misuse his water. This was the same penalty that the old mayordomos used to make sure people used the water correctly. We thanked him for his time and continued on our way.

Watching him close the check gate reminds us of one of the amazing engineering feats of these old acequias: they depended on only gravity to move the waters. There are no pumps or other mechanical devices. From as far back as the Middle Ages in Spain, people understood that water would run downhill on its own; all the builders of the acequias had to do was figure out how to make a downhill flow with the system of gates. The farmer

Ancient orchard at Gutierrez-Hubbel House. *Authors' collection.*

Gate opening an ancient acequia. *Courtesy of Patty Carman.*

raising the depth of the water here on the Pajaritas Acequia was intuitively building on a long tradition of fluid dynamics.

We see a number of domestic animals in the farms along the ditch, and all of them depend on the water. A curious sheep wanders over to see who we are. This sheep is a remnant of the huge flocks that accompanied the Spanish settlers along the Camino Royale. The Bernalillo County shield (shown in this book's introduction) displays sheep as a reminder that herding was the main occupation of the area's early inhabitants. This lone animal will provide enough wool for domestic consumption. He did have a noisy sheepdog to keep him company.

We see other animals along the way—chickens, roosters and a penned pig whose owner told us he had misbehaved and that was why he was caged for the day. He usually roams free. As we wandered off, I was left wondering what kind of mischief the pig got into.

We reach a road and turn east to walk toward Isleta Boulevard, and then we turn north to head back to the Gutiérrez-Hubbel House. We walk through the parking lot, through the little plaza where we started our walk, and head over to the house.

At first glance, the house is unremarkable, a one-story structure with a deep, shady porch facing the plaza. But when we look more closely at the architecture, we can see the influential elements that have continued to be used in New Mexico.

The house covers over 5,700 square feet and was built with the traditional flat roof. The original house consisted of eight rooms. More rooms were added later, as the family grew large and needed more space. The house was built with 28-inch-thick walls that insulated the house from the summer heat and winter cold. The tall 11-foot ceilings allow the hot air to rise, cooling the people who gather in the rooms.

The walls are made of sod block and adobe covered with stucco. The *viga* (log) roof beams support the structure. Core samples show that the beams were cut between 1850 and 1859, testifying to the soundness of this kind of construction. As we enter, we can see the great room that has been restored to its original style. The beautiful wooden floors, stucco walls, great fireplace and log ceilings show us what it would have been like when this house hosted political and social functions and became an envied hacienda of the Albuquerque area.

The adobe and stucco flat-roofed house displays traditional Spanish and Native architecture. However, the easterner Hubbell brought some of his own ideas to the architecture. There is white Greek Revival trim around

Interior of the Guttierrez-Hubbell House. *Authors' collection.*

the windows and doors, and this feature marked the house as something different. This is called the "Territorial" style in New Mexico, and it is linked with the arrival of the United States in the region. Families who built in the Territorial style showed the family was not only fashionable but also belonged to the highest social class.

As we walk back to the car, we think about how visiting this house, its fields and orchards and its life-giving acequia, takes us back to the origins of

Albuquerque settlement. Here, at the beginning of the Spanish settlement, the region was marked by a blending of cultures, plants and animals. None of these would have taken hold without the work to divert the waters of the Rio Grande into the acequias.

It is spring now, so we will walk along some acequias that will show us new growth, young animals and rushing waters. We will follow the continued acquisition of new animals and invasive plants that marked the beginnings of the settlements. The easements along all these ditches allow us to walk and share the living waters that feed the region as we enjoy this remarkable resource of the Rio Grande valley.

PART II

SPRING

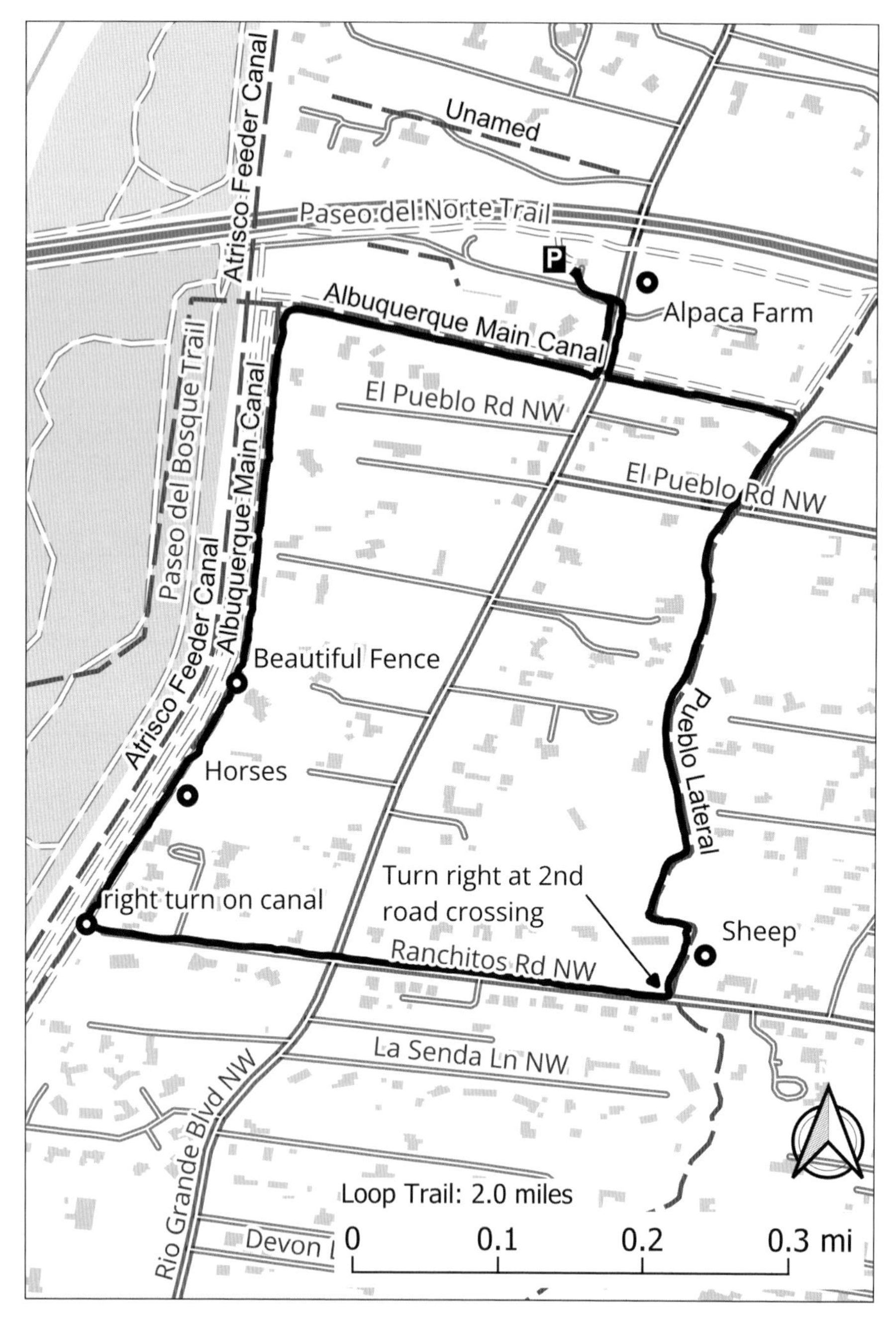

Roger Cardon.

4

SPRING ALONG THE SHINING RIVER

It is spring in Albuquerque. The temperature says it is in the fifties, but the sun that is now high in the sky spreads so much warmth that we can walk without jackets. In the early spring, the acequias begin to fill to prepare for the new growth. We head to the neighborhood of Los Ranchos to trace the beginnings of spring along these irrigation ditches.

Los Ranchos is a village in Bernalillo County on the east side of the Rio Grande. It is surrounded on three sides by the larger city of Albuquerque, but it retains its rural quality that has marked it for centuries. The first Indigenous pueblos were established by 600 CE, and by 1200 CE, there were major sites along the Rio Grande to take advantage of the precious water. The largest of these pueblos was located in today's Rio Rancho, a four-square-mile oasis outside of the growing city.

When the Spanish arrived, Hernando de Alvarado saw the region in 1540, and he described the area as a "broad valley planted with fields of maize and dotted with cottonwood groves."[15] By 1750, the Los Ranchos Plaza was established, and the community began to grow. Residents maintained the acequias that the Spaniards dug, and they incorporated the Pueblo irrigation ditches, but just like river valleys elsewhere, the land was prone to flooding. Devastating floods during the late nineteenth century destroyed farms and the village itself, and that rich farmland became more alkaline, threatening any agriculture.

The region was saved for agriculture in the early twentieth century, when the network of dams, levees, drains and irrigation ditches tamed the Rio

Grande, no longer allowing for spring floods. Families moved in to add ranches and farms to the region. However, residents were concerned that the growing population of Albuquerque would overwhelm the community of Los Ranchos. Therefore, in 1958, the residents incorporated the village, protecting it from expanding urban sprawl. This area is one of the least-developed sections of the valley and retains a beautiful, rural quality.

To begin our walk, we start at the Shining River parking area to access the Bosque along the acequias. Before we start, I wonder why this is called the "Shining River"? As we will see, it is beautiful, but it doesn't seem more shining than other parts of the ditches. It turns out the name has an interesting history of its own, tied to a remarkable woman who lived in Los Ranchos.

In 1976, Kathryn "Kit" Sargeant moved to Albuquerque. Kit was an archaeologist and advocate for historic preservation; she was also a community advocate and organizer who left her mark on Los Ranchos. As she grew interested in the history of Los Ranchos, she wanted to preserve the river, the acequias and the history of the region. In 1986, Sargeant published a book based on her conversations with the area's residents. It is called *Shining River, Precious Land: An Oral History of Albuquerque's North Valley*. Sargeant died in 2001, but her legacy is preserved in the Shining River Open Space and access to the Bosque with its wonderful running water.

We start our walk at the Shining River Open Space parking lot. We walk to the stop sign on Rio Grande Boulevard. Straight across the street, we can see an alpaca farm, with several alpacas enjoying the sun.

Alpacas are raised for their wonderful wool, which is softer and more durable than sheep wool. Alpacas were first imported into the United States in 1984, and alpaca farms have spread widely all over the United States. Alpaca farms were introduced to New Mexico in about 2000, and garments made from this wool are highly valued—and expensive. This farm represents some of the new animals that have been introduced to this area.

As we leave the farm, we turn east. Shortly afterward, we come to the Albuquerque Main Canal and go left. This canal goes east and then takes a sharp turn north. We turn right (south) and follow the Pueblo Lateral. As we enter these acequias that have been here much longer than the alpacas, we can move back in time and see the farms that have been using this water for centuries.

We enter the narrow dirt ditch path that weaves through the homes and farms that line the waterway. As we stroll along the narrow ease way next to the ditch, the first thing we notice are the sounds of spring. The water

Alpaca on the farm near the Shining River. *Courtesy of Carmen Caswell.*

is rushing, the March wind is rustling the early leaves, doves are cooing and crows are shouting. Even frogs begin to croak. We notice some robins lingering here on their way north for the summer. The silent winter has lifted, and we love the music of the spring woods. Kit Sargeant included a record of children's songs in her book on the Shining River, as the children of the community came out to the playgrounds and chanted songs as they played.[16] In their chants, the children sang of the Bosque waking from the winter. The playgrounds are too far from this acequia for us to hear the children's songs, but we can enjoy the other sounds of spring.

The acequia curves along between the homes and fields that will be watered by the newly flowing stream.

It is narrow here, but the old cottonwoods cling tenaciously to the narrow bank. Their deep roots hold them even as they seem to cling perilously to the edge. They've been here for about a century, so we don't have to worry about them falling in.

As we walk, we can see the irrigation gates that stand open and will later be closed to divert the water into the nearby fields. The gates are in good repair. We notice that there is cement lining the ditch close to the gates, to keep the wood from eroding out with the water, but the ditch itself is left bare. The moving waters will help restore the aquifer along here.

As we move along the acequia, we notice a small white truck with the logo of the Middle Rio Grande Conservancy District on the side. This is

Acequia gate with water rushing. *Authors' collection.*

the ditch rider's truck, and he is here to open the irrigation ditch at the top of the acequia to release more water. As he opens the gate, the water rushes in.

He kindly takes time to talk to us a bit about his job. In 1923, the conservancy district took over the job of monitoring the acequias from the community-led mayordomo system. The entire system of flood control of the Rio Grande required a more centralized system to decide where and when the waters would run. At that time, the ditch riders took over the role of monitoring the hundreds of miles of water that supply the Middle Rio Grande. We imagine that in 1923, the ditch riders rode horses as they moved along the acequias, but now, they use small trucks.

The ditch rider did tell us he thought of himself as the heir to the mayordomo. He was in charge of making sure the community of water, plants, animals and humans thrived together. His job is to see that the waters run properly, the ditches stay in repair and the irrigation gates open on an appropriate schedule. It's a fine, important job, and we said our goodbyes as he got in his truck to leave. We continue our walk along the ditch.

The community of animals in the valley is made up of much more than the native porcupines and beavers. When the Spanish arrived in the sixteenth century, they brought their own animals—horses, cattle, sheep and goats. These were quickly assimilated to the land, raised and enjoyed by Indigenous peoples as well as settlers. Here in the village of Los Ranchos, which proudly preserves its rural character, we find these animals well represented. We turn right to follow the ditch. Along here, the waterway is called the Pueblo Acequia, and we wind along the curved ditch.

Along the edge of the acequia, we peer into a sheltered pen and find two sheep. These are the old wool-bearers that were here long before the new upstart alpacas. These sheep are heavily laden with their winter coats of wool, waiting to be shorn soon. The wool will be woven into one of the many products that are abundant here. The sheep watch us placidly as they lift their heads from their food trough. They are not bothered by us, but that is the nature of sheep.

This two-mile walk takes us along the Pueblo Acequia south to Ranchitos Road. There, we turn right to walk west. We pass more homes with the kind of spacious land that Los Ranchos is noted for and see more and more domestic animals. Herds of horses are in the local corrals, eating hay since the new spring grass isn't quite long enough for grazing.

When we reach the end of Ranchitos Road, we turn right to walk along the Albuquerque Main Canal that parallels the Atrisco Feeder. We head north and can see both ditches as we walk, and a man on horseback rides along the Atrisco Feeder. He's watching his phone. Is it OK to text while horseback riding? I suppose so. The horse won't crash into anything.

As we meander, we see more horses grazing in the fields near the ditch. We also see cows in a pen nearby. I wonder if these are Criollo cattle, a breed

Acequia gate open. *Authors' collection.*

descended from the first cattle brought to Mexico by Hernán Cortés. This breed of cattle is being extensively studied by scientists. They are able to range over larger areas than other domestic cattle and travel longer through the dry desert regions of the Southwest than more highly bred cattle that were later imported from England. They have a reduced water dependency and are looked on as an important resource during the increasingly dry periods associated with climate change. These cows look simply content as they relax in the shade of the barn, blissfully unaware of their significant biological heritage.

As we walk out of the Pueblo Acequia, we are out of the narrow ditch, and we can see the valley open up, the Sandia Mountains visible to the east. While we are in the sheltered acequia, it was easy to forget that we are part of this great valley. Here in this open vista, we see one of our favorite marks of spring: a beautiful crabapple tree in flower, framed by the Sandias in the background.

Spring is here.

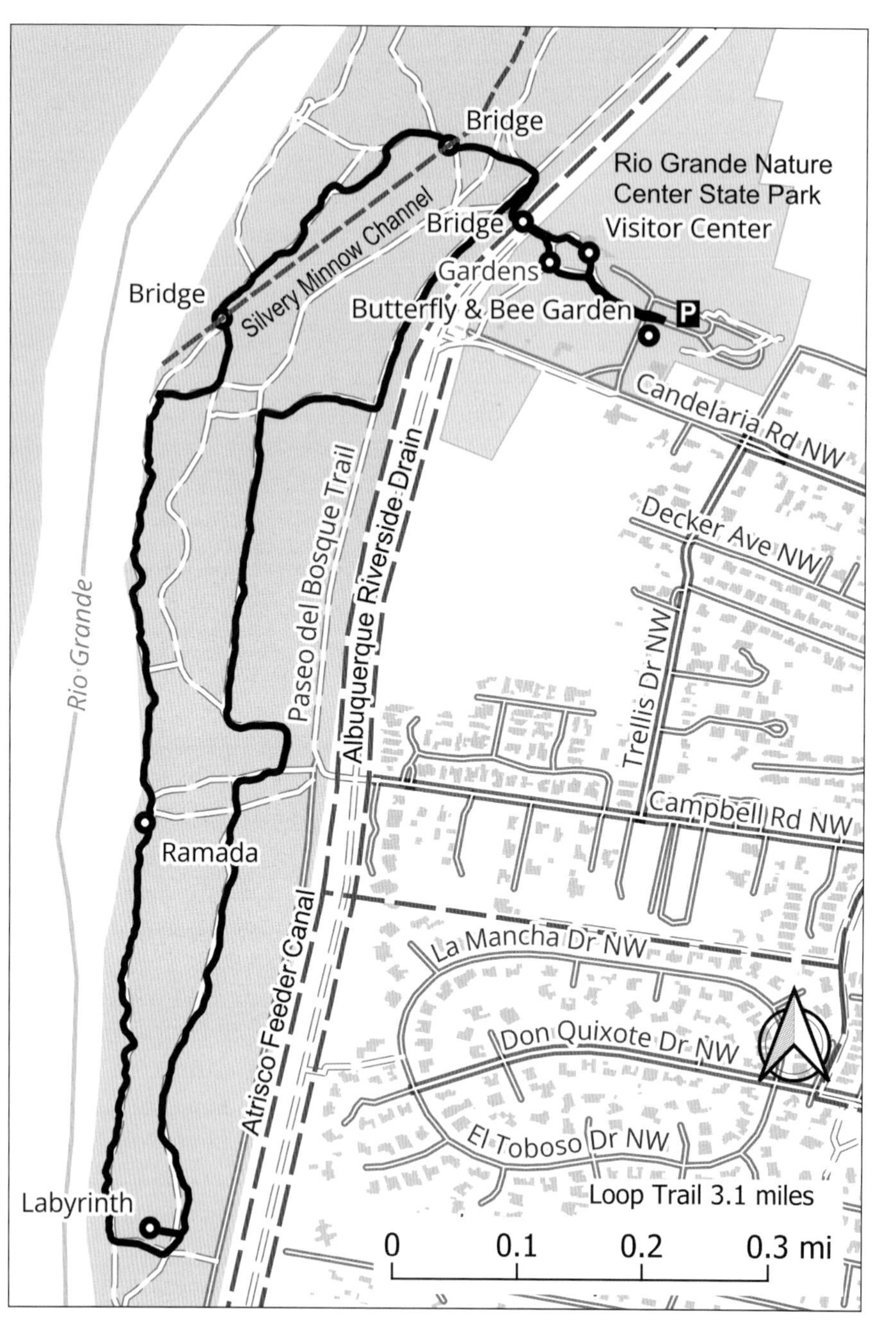

Roger Cardon.

5

ACEQUIAS BEHIND THE NATURE CENTER

The cottonwood forest and its adjacent acequias and lateral ditches form one of the remarkable natural settings in the city of Albuquerque. Of course, the State of New Mexico wants people to be able to appreciate this wonderful resource, and to help with this, the state opened a nature center. This Rio Grande Nature Center State Park was established in 1982. It is a thirty-eight-acre wildlife preserve that satisfies several goals: about two-thirds of the grounds are set aside as habitat for wildlife. There is also a visitors' center, gardens and an education building. In addition, the nature center is adjacent to a building that houses a nonprofit organization that rehabilitates wildlife and releases healed animals back into the wild. The park has its own paths but also offers access to the Bosque to walk on trails going both north and south.

Today, for our walk, we will start at the visitors' center. We park in the lot after paying the three-dollar parking fee. Before we go into the nature center building, we stroll over to the butterfly garden adjacent to the parking lot. Here, there are extensive native plants and information about the butterflies, birds and pollinators in the region. Since it is spring, the hummingbirds have migrated back and are eagerly looking for the native flowers. As is always the case with these tiny birds, they fly rapidly around, always looking for more pollen to satisfy their high metabolism.

All these flower beds are designed to offer flowers to support the many pollinators that are essential for the health of the area's ecosystem, and this effort isn't limited to the nature center. In 2012, Albuquerque received a designation as a "Bee City USA." This certification demonstrates that the city is committed to creating an environment that will support all pollinators. This commitment means that Albuquerque will reduce harmful chemicals and create programs that will teach people about bees.[17] The nature center is part of this program, and we can see this in its native plantings as well as its educational signage. As we strolled through the gardens, we learned a lot about the native pollinators and their diets.

One of the displays that encourages the presence of bees is a bee house that provides space for the insects. There are 3,600 bee species in New Mexico, and about one-third of these are solitary bees and wasps (unlike the honeybees that live in communities). This bee house is for the solitary bees. A female bee lays her eggs along with pollen reserves in one of these small holes. Then she fills in the hole with garden debris (leaves and sticks), leaving the eggs to hatch and produce new bees. Many people have started to include these attractive bee houses in their gardens to support the solitary pollinators. It is this kind of encouragement that has made Albuquerque a certified Bee City USA.

It is tempting to stay in these gardens, but we have to move on. As we turn toward the nature center building, we are welcomed by an unusual entryway. The door is designed to force visitors to enter through an eight-foot-diameter drainage culvert that forms a tunnel entry into the building. This was designed to remind the visitors of the essential connection between the nature park and the water that feeds it.

The nature center itself is a well-designed center for education. As we enter the visitor center, we are greeted by a series of vertical, eight-foot-high water-filled tubes around a viewing area. Like the culvert entryway, these tubes also remind visitors of the importance of water to this whole ecosystem. There is a pump here, too, that allows visitors to pump water up from the aquifer to show the second source of water in addition to the water from the river.

The visitors' center has a series of exhibits about the local plants and animals and a discovery room with hands-on exhibits for children. We particularly like a separate viewing room where we can look over one of the ponds. We saw geese, turtles and ducks, but most interesting is that there are microphones outside the building so we can hear the sounds of the birds as we watch them. There is also a nice, small shop inside.

We tear ourselves away from the building to head out the back. Our goal is to walk along the acequias that border the Rio Grande, which lies about half a mile due west from the nature center. We first reach one of the viewing

Bee house at the nature center. *Authors' collection.*

blinds that overlook a pond, where we can see water birds and turtles. Many visitors were taking pictures through the small windows in the blind.

We cross the Albuquerque Riverside Drain by a small bridge and then turn south to walk along a little acequia that runs parallel to the Atrisco Feeder lateral. It is early spring, and the cottonwoods, a tree that blooms late, are just now beginning to sprout their light green leaves. The light shines

Above: Culvert entry to the nature center. *Authors' collection.*

Opposite: Cormorant diving along the Silvery Minnow Channel. *Authors' collection.*

through the trees in a way that signals spring; in summer, the dark green leaves will offer more shade. For now, we appreciate the warm sun shining through, since the spring temperatures are still a little cool.

As we walk along the trail, we suddenly spot a nest fairly low in an evergreen tree, and we were able to get a picture of it. The bottom photograph on page 100 shows this nest with three fledgling thrushes inside. They are almost ready to leave the nest because it is full and crowded, but they still wait for their mother to return with food. Hermit thrushes like these are common in New Mexico, and they nest on the edges of forest trails. They feed on insects, like ants and flies, and sometimes seeds if nothing else is available. The mother must have her hands full foraging for these large, healthy nestlings.

Before we go much farther along the ditch, we see a pair of cormorants diving for fish. We can briefly see little minnows in their beaks. They swallow them quickly before they warm their feathers resting on a branch.

The cormorants remind us that there is more to this ecosystem than the animals and plants we can see. On our previous walks, we have noticed how the waters of the Rio Grande have been controlled with dams and acequias. It's made wonderful recreational and agricultural use of the waters. But like all good things, they come with a cost. These improvements caused a grave impact on the small Rio Grande silvery minnow.

The little ditch that we are walking along is called the Silvery Minnow Channel to remind walkers of the importance of this little fish. This fish, which is between two and four inches long, was once one of the most common species in the Rio Grande. But by 1994, it was listed as endangered. The alteration of the river system stopped the spring runoff that had once triggered spawning for the fish. Furthermore, their habitat was degraded, and the construction of the dams seriously interfered with the minnows' life cycle. In addition, the flow of water through the acequias and back into the river brought pollutants into the river that further degraded the population. In 1994, the fish were found in only 5 percent of its former habitat. Between 1999 and 2010, there were a series of lawsuits brought forward to protect the fish. However, it is a difficult situation, since so many people (and other animals, for that matter) use the diverted waters.

Finally, in 2000, the U.S. Fish and Wildlife Service devised a plan to increase the silvery minnow population; humans created the problem, and it's up to us to solve it. Each spring, biologists collect minnow eggs from Elephant Butte Reservoir in southern New Mexico, where these collections won't disturb the upstream population. They are then brought to the Albuquerque BioPark (near Tingley Beach). There, the Aquatic Conservation Facility raises the hatchlings then releases them into the Rio Grande. Each year, biologists release about twenty-five thousand minnows into the river.[18] These efforts have helped, but the little silvery fish remains endangered. The twenty-five thousand minnows swim south in the river, and some are diverted into the laterals and acequias. Some even feed hungry cormorants.

We continue to walk south as we talk about the little fish, and we enjoy the beginnings of spring. Some spring wildflowers have begun to grow. We see a large patch of a beautiful orange flower. This is a globe mallow, a brightly colored desert plant. Just when we think this high desert is dominated by the browns and dark greens of the year-round plants, these seasonal wonders appear!

As always, it's peaceful walking along the ditch. There are a few people with their binoculars watching the birds; the nature center claims there are over three hundred species of birds visible here. My bird-watching skills extend only to the waterbirds that float along the acequia and, now, the little thrushes in the nest, but we can see other more advanced birders increasing their count.

We reach the Rio Grande and stroll along its banks. As we are admiring the river, we reach a ramada, a Southwest term for a roofed structure with

Labyrinth south of the nature center. *Authors' collection.*

open sides. The term comes from the Spanish term for "branch" or "arbor," and these buildings were named for the temporary structures that were erected to shade people from the desert heat. As is typical, this ramada is roofed with open sides. It has a number of logs for us to sit on and rest by the river before we continue on. We leave the riverbank and head east, back into the woods.

Walking through the woods is always a peaceful, meditative experience. The Japanese call this experience "forest bathing," or *shinrin-yoku*. As mentioned in this book's introduction, studies have shown that walking in the woods, feeling the breeze, inhaling the sweet smells of the trees and plants, has lots of positive health benefits. Not only does this activity alleviate stress, but it also increases anti-inflammatory responses in our bodies. As we were reflecting on whether our meandering was inducing a relaxing meditative state, we came upon a surprising find: a labyrinth laid out near our path.

Labyrinths are circular paths laid out on the ground that guide a walker to the center. There is a long history of labyrinths being constructed throughout the world. The idea of such a path is for walkers to focus on entering the center of the circle, concentrating on negotiating the complicated form which calms the mind (much like a forest walk). When they reach the center, they are supposedly in a meditative state. They are supposed to have reached their own center as well as the center of the circle. There are over six thousand labyrinths listed in the Worldwide Labyrinth Locator, which shows how ubiquitous this form has become, though our labyrinth isn't listed.[19] The most famous labyrinths include those at Chartres Cathedral in France, St. George's Cathedral in Cape Town and many others. Our small labyrinth is about forty feet in diameter, and it is a surprising find. The first Saturday in May is National Labyrinth Day; we are early since we are walking in April, but we will try it anyway.

This labyrinth was laid out around an ancient stump in the center. It's been here for years, but there is no way to find out how old it is. The labyrinth is made of pieces of wood, and it has been repaired several times, as we can see with the newer branches that have been inserted. We gave it a try and walked through. It wasn't as easy as it looks; it is easy to become distracted and step over a dead end. It takes full concentration and patience. One person made it successfully, and he sat on the stump, enjoying the feel of success—and perhaps the centering.

After playing around with the labyrinth for a while, we headed back north to the nature center. Instead of going straight back to the car, we wandered again through the gardens that exhibit native plants and grasses. There are benches to sit and relax on while admiring all the plantings. It's spring, so flowers are beginning to bloom, and the native grasses are swaying in the breeze.

This nature center is a wonderful resource for the city of Albuquerque. It is good for the native plants, birds and pollinators and animals, and it is wonderful for walkers who want to enjoy the cottonwood forest.

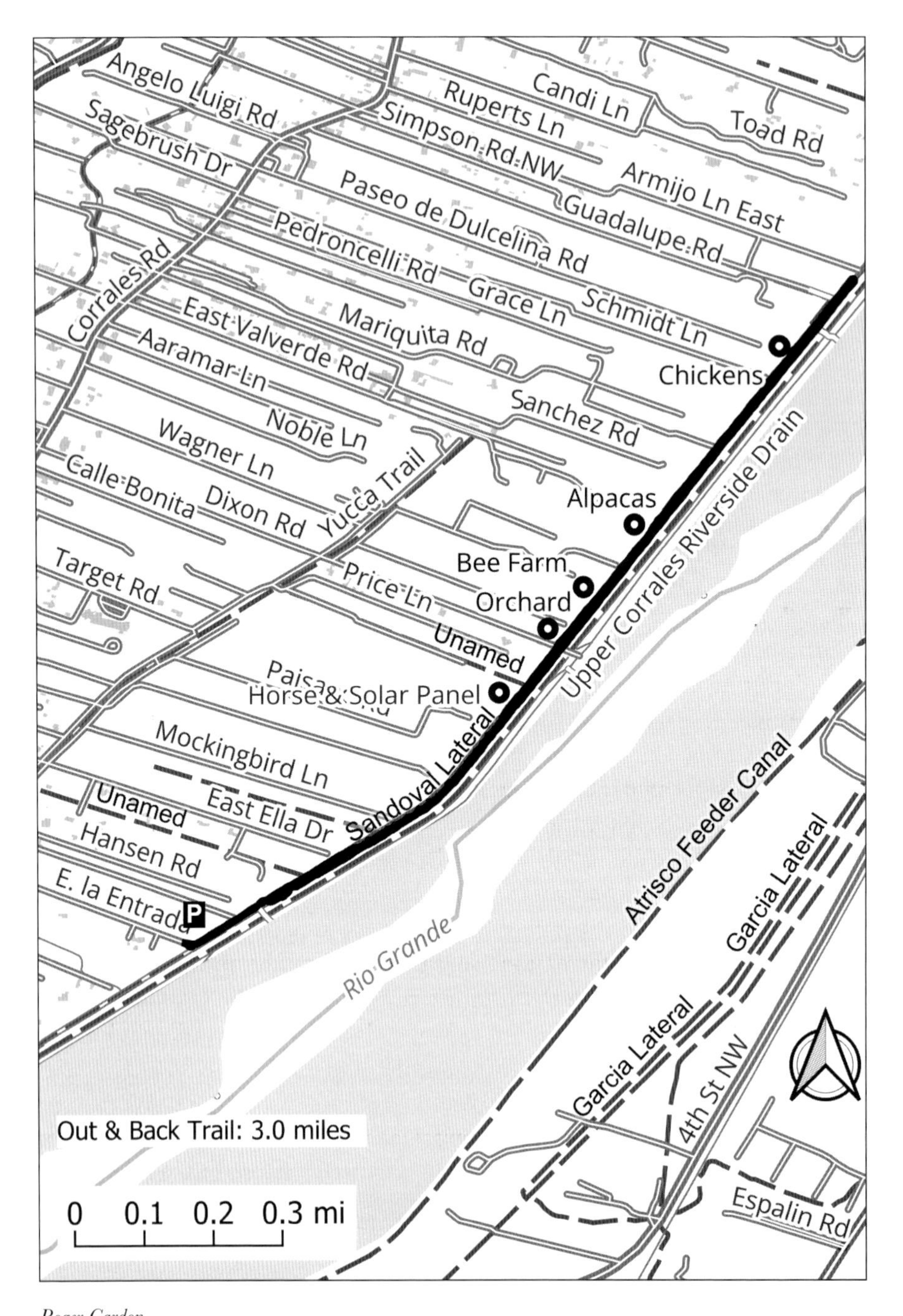

Roger Cardon.

6

THE AGRICULTURAL LANDS OF CORRALES

Corrales is a village in southern Sandoval County, just north of Bernalillo County and Albuquerque. While it is in the greater Albuquerque area, Corrales preserves its own character based on its long history. This special character of Corrales makes it a perfect place to look at and think about the impact of the movement of people, plants and animals through this region. The land has been transformed, and we can see the traces of this evolution here.

Corrales is located along the Rio Grande, and because of its fertile alluvial soil, it was first settled before 500 CE by the Tiguex First Nation. One thousand years later, the Spanish colonists settled the area, using it for agriculture and animal husbandry. The name Corrales means "corrals," which preserves the memory of the livestock ranching that marked the region. The first transformation we can see from the movement of the Tiguex to the Spanish is in the people's relationship to the land itself. Both had to use the water for irrigation and moved the water accordingly, but the Tiguex used the land; they didn't own it. The Spanish owned the land, and that meant they put fences around plots to mark their ownership. We can see the fences and walls that clearly separate each person's property. However, the Spanish also recognized that the water had to be shared among everyone. The acequias that build on the Tiguex irrigation lands preserve this idea.

The current village of Corrales was incorporated in 1971, and because it has preserved its character for so many years, it was selected in CNN Money's "List of the 100 Best Places to Live" in 2007.[20] The ancient settlement of the village makes it an interesting place to walk through the town. There is the Church of San Ysidro that was built in 1868 and many old buildings that now serve as restaurants and art galleries. Today, however, we will explore the farms and corrals that encircle this wonderful village.

In addition to holding farmland and livestock, the village of Corrales has set aside land along some of the ditches as a conservation area. This land is called the Corrales Bosque Preserve, a narrow strip that contains the cottonwood forest and related riparian habitats. The spirit of this preserved area continues the idea that the water in the acequias belongs to everyone, and the Bosque is a continuation of the preserved woodlands that we have enjoyed farther south in Albuquerque. In 1978, this strip of land was declared a protected area that the village oversees as a natural wildlife preserve. Like the Bosque elsewhere, this is a valuable corridor for birds, both nesting and migrating. Today, we will walk along this Bosque trail to focus on the neighboring farms.

One of the many ways Corrales sets itself apart from the neighboring Bernalillo County is through its management of its water resources. Corrales doesn't have a centralized water system; many homes have to install their own wells and sewage disposal systems. However, the village carefully stewards the extensive acequia system that maintains the rural character of the village. The water is managed by the Middle Rio Grande Conservancy District (MRGCD) that controls the water in Bernalillo County, but the conservancy district works closely with village officials. At the beginning of each season, the water managers decide when to begin the irrigation season.

In 2024, after studying the area's soil conditions, water and temperatures, the managers decided to start the season early. These shifts in timing are going on everywhere and are markers of the warming climate. Beginning at the end of February, managers began to send some water through the ditches to flush the canals and make sure the system works properly. The first water deliveries start in April, so we will walk these irrigation ditches in April to see what spring looks like as the water starts to flow to the fields.

Once we enter Corrales, we turn right on the East La Estrada Road, right before the senior center, and park at the end of the road where it connects to the ditch. Then we walk north along the Sandoval Lateral. This acequia parallels The Corrales Drain, and both run parallel to the Rio Grande. The Sandoval Lateral serves as the feeder for the irrigation ditches that supply this rich agricultural land. The water flows rapidly south as it heads back to the Rio Grande. We will walk north along this ditch for about one and a half miles and then turn around to come back, making this walk about three

Corrales acequia watering the farmlands and orchards. *Authors' collection.*

miles long, but walkers can choose to go as far as they like and still enjoy this water corridor.

We are walking along this acequia at the end of April, so we can already see the results of the water management water release. Even though we can see the gates open to allow the water to move, the water in this acequia is low, halfway down its highwater mark. This means that the fields are already receiving their water allocation, and the bright green fields along our walk reflect the movement of the water.

As we look at the well-tended farms along the ditch, it is obvious that this is horse country. When the Spanish first brought horses to New Mexico, they flourished, and people love them. Some of the properties have large homes made of the traditional stucco, while others have smaller structures, but almost all of them have the horses that have filled the corrals of this region for centuries.

One farm links the past with the future in a striking way. We saw a horse grazing peacefully in front of large solar panels, shown in the top image on page 67. Like so many states, New Mexico has offered incentives to move to solar energy. Albuquerque averages 280 sunny days a year, so solar energy is an excellent alternative. This farm is looking toward the future of energy while preserving the heritage of horse husbandry that has marked this region for centuries.

We also see other animals that have been here since the Spanish colonization. A large flock of chickens enjoy the shade of a large cottonwood as they search for grain and grubs. Of course, dogs everywhere guard their owners' property, barking at us as we walk by. I can't imagine this land without these animals that were imported by the Spanish and have since made New Mexico home.

We see a newly imported animal as well—a herd of alpacas populate one farm. These twentieth-century imports have slowly started to replace herds of sheep, as new farmers appreciate the alpaca wool.

As we walk along, we see a farm dedicated to producing honey. It is wonderful to see these bee houses erected to raise European honeybees.

The Spanish brought these bees with them to pollinate the new crops they had also brought from Europe. These bees are not like the solitary bees we saw in the nature center in the last chapter. These bees live in colonies and have been domesticated for centuries. They are willing to share their honey with us as they live in houses we provide.

In 2006, when honeybee colonies started disappearing all over the country in what became known as "colony collapse disorder," everyone who was

Left: Corrales horse grazing in front of solar panels. *Authors' collection.*

Below: Corrales European honeybee hives. *Authors' collection.*

paying attention became concerned. Our food supply and flowering plants depend on pollinators, including honeybees. This was when Albuquerque became dedicated to preserving all pollinators—native and imported—and became a certified Bee City USA.

As we walk, we don't want to neglect noticing the plants that also came with the Spanish and transformed the land. Since it is spring, one of the first plants we notice is the humble but ubiquitous dandelion. This European plant has spread all over North America, much to the bane of gardeners but to the pleasure of those who enjoy dandelion green salad and dandelion wine.

Another farm is watering a large, healthy-looking apple orchard. The only apple native to North America is a small crabapple, and the Spanish didn't bring apples in their settlement. All the delicious apples we see at the farmers' markets and grocery stores were brought with settlers from the eastern United States in the nineteenth century. This orchard shows another layer of plants that accompanied waves of settlers as they slowly spread across the land.

As you can tell, most of the farms along this route have open fences that allow us to see into their lands and admire their plants and animals. Some people, however, prefer more privacy. Periodically, we come across a fence that completely shields a yard. These fences are often made of simple bark-covered narrow logs. One such fence has a surprise: a yellow Lady Banks' climbing rose escaped from the fence and is blooming beautifully along our path. This beautiful rose originally came from the highlands of China, where the altitude matches that of Albuquerque. Settlers eventually imported these beautiful roses that thrive here in the high desert. It was a treat to see it.

It is easy to be distracted by beautiful roses and healthy apple trees, but we are quickly reminded that the dominant plant in the Bosque, the great cottonwood, is a native. It was here before the Spanish and before the First Nation tribes arrived. It is spring, and the cottonwoods are beginning to seed. White fluffs of what appear to be cotton blow through the air. It is easy to see how the cottonwoods got their name. What is this cotton?

Male and female flowers grow on separate trees, and only large cottonwoods can bloom. Male trees bear flowers in long red clusters called catkins. These produce pollen, which is carried on the wind—and spring in New Mexico brings a lot of wind! Once a female flower is pollinated, the female flowers develop capsules containing tiny seeds with cottony plumes. Each female tree produces thousands of these cottony capsules that flow on

Apple orchard in Corrales. *Authors' collection.*

the wind. By late spring and early summer, so many of these plumes float on the winds that they look like snow.

Before we diverted the river and regulated its flow, the cottonwood seeds' disbursement coincided with the river flooding its banks. To germinate, cottonwood seeds need to land on wet, sunny sandbars that are left as the river recedes. Now that the river is controlled, most of the seeds will not land somewhere suitable for germination. We see an old cottonwood surrounded by plumes of seeds so deep it looks like a snow cover. Occasionally, the flow of the river shifts, providing a sunny, sandy bank for seeds to take hold and put down their deep roots to go down into the groundwater. But this is unusual. Now, forest managers plant seedlings to replace cottonwoods in open spaces to preserve this ancient habitat.

We started this walk thinking about the Spanish colonization and the plants and animals that transformed this land when they arrived. But as we arrive back at our cars, we are reminded of the age-old land that is preserved here in the Bosque. This environment was shaped by the free-flowing river and the cottonwood trees that blow white plumes through the air every spring.

PART III

SUMMER

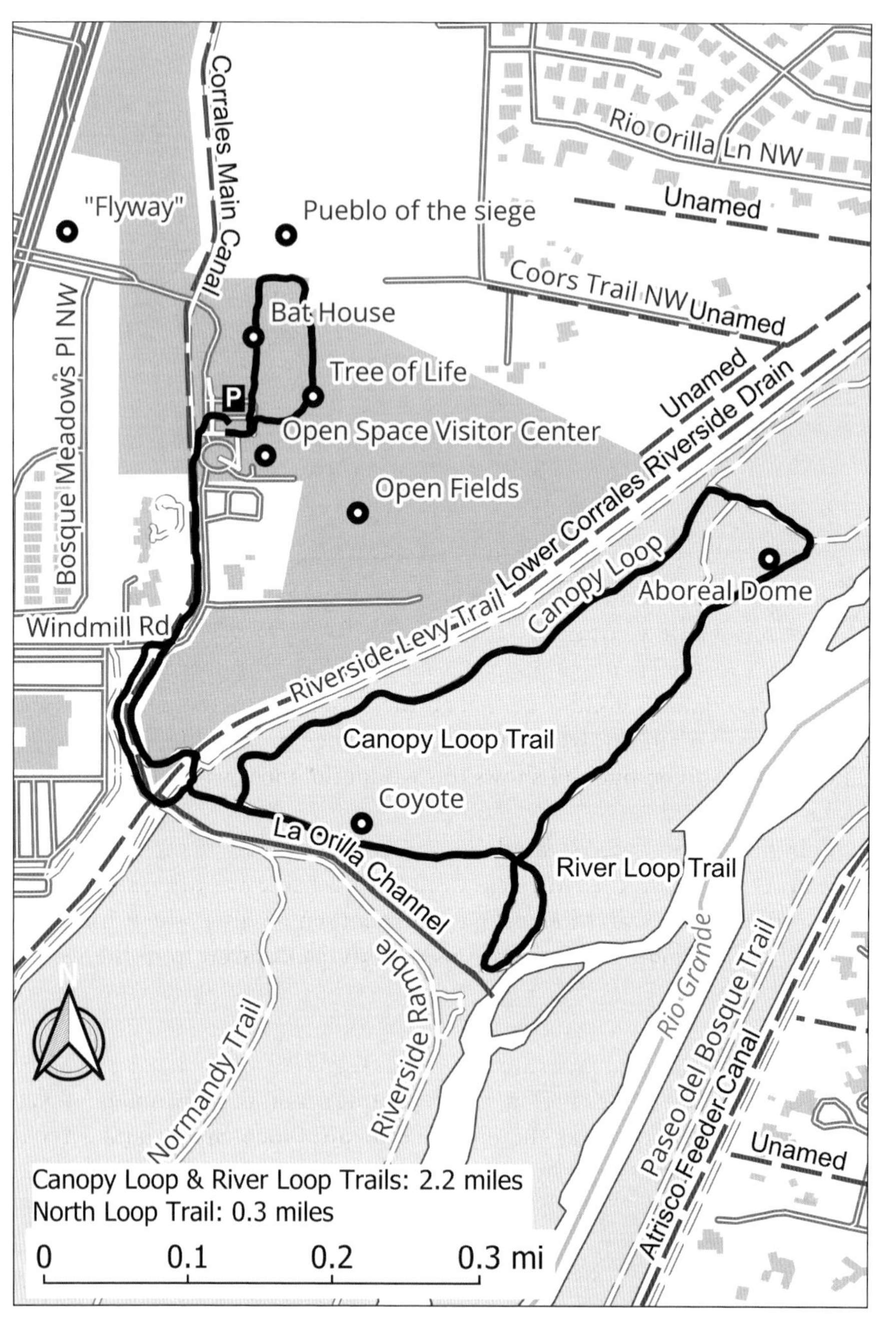

Roger Cardon.

7

WALKING TO THE OPEN SPACE VISITOR CENTER

Our destination today is the West Side Open Space Visitors' Center that is located along the Corrales Riverside Drain that runs parallel to the west side of the Rio Grande. As we drive north along Coors Boulevard, we turn to the right on Bosque Meadows Road, into the entrance of the Open Space's visitors' center. At the turn is a striking piece of public art: tall spikes in an array that mark the entrance road to the Open Space. The photograph on page 74 shows this wonderful piece with the mountains in the background.

This installation was created by Robert Wilson, who competed in a land art competition that was held in 2009. The task was to create art that "incorporates landscape in one way or another." Wilson drew from the Bosque by creating the installation using jetty jacks taken from the woods that had once been used to hold back the Rio Grande floods but are no longer needed. By moving all these jetty jacks, he preserved the memory of their use. He organized them in a way that suggested cranes flying gracefully in their migration to this region. The resulting—and prize-winning—piece is called *Flyway* and marks the entrance to the Open Space lands. Yet it marks something else as well, a sad part of the history of this land.

Behind the *Flyway* piece, there is an expanse of empty land; in consultation with tribal leaders, New Mexico has agreed to leave this area untouched because it was the site of an ancient massacre. There is no sign describing the events on the fence surrounding the vacant, overgrown land. Visitors have to enter the visitors' center to read about the history and find remnants

Flyway sculpture at the Open Space. *Courtesy of Toni Slimp.*

of arrowheads and crossbow pieces to recall the events. The land here is left as a silent graveyard of remembrance.

In 1540, Francisco Vázques de Coronado led a small expedition north from Mexico to look for the mythical "Seven Cities of Gold." He led about 400 Spanish soldiers, accompanied by some 1,500 Mexican Native allies, and his expedition got as far as modern Kansas. (Needless to say, he found no cities of gold.) Along the Rio Grande, Coronado went to war with the Pueblos. Texts describing these battles tell of a great siege that took place at the largest of the pueblos, and archaeologist Matt Schmader makes an excellent case that this land behind the *Flyway* sculpture is the "pueblo of the siege."[21]

This pueblo is now called Piedras Marcadas Pueblo, or the "Village of the Marked Rocks," because of its proximity to the mesa that has many petroglyphs dating from this era. It was a huge village, covering some thirty thousand acres that held multistory edifices surrounding plazas and markets. When Coronado attacked, the Spaniards besieged the pueblo for between fifty and eighty days. The texts describe several attacks at the walls that the Natives repelled.

However, while the Natives held off the Spanish forces, they ran out of water. They tried to dig a well inside the fortified compound, but it collapsed, killing perhaps thirty of the Native peoples. The pueblo was destroyed and descended into rubble as the Spanish moved on. But the land remembered the violence.

In 1988, the city declared the land sacred and purchased it as part of the Open Spaces of Albuquerque. The land has since been preserved in remembrance of those who died here. When we look at the *Flyway* installation, we can't help but see the spears that recall the ancient violence in this space. But art is often in the eye of the beholder, and the stunning installation marks both the past, the violent spears and the jetty jacks, and the present, the path of migrating birds.

What allowed Albuquerque to purchase and preserve both the sacred space and all the adjacent Open Spaces is that this is a city with a deep appreciation for the beautiful outdoor spaces that weave through the city. Beginning in the 1960s, city leaders worked to preserve these Open Spaces and highlight their value for recreation. However, they also wanted to recognize the intrinsic value of the natural spaces themselves. In 1969, the City Goals Committee wrote that its goal was to "preserve the unique natural features of the metropolitan area by achieving a pattern of development and open space respecting the river, land, mesa, mountains, volcanoes, and arroyos." Since then, Albuquerque acquired over twenty-four thousand acres of Open Space land and established a permanent fund for the management of these lands.

The city owns or manages over 30,000 acres of Open Space lands, distributed on the east and west sides of the city and incorporating the volcanoes and the mesas. Throughout this book, we have focused on the 5,129 acres in the Bosque and the valley.[22]

The Open Space Visitors' Center is one part of these extensive lands. It consists of agricultural lands, managed for the benefit of migrating birds; a few miles of trails leading through the adjacent Bosque; and a visitors' center that has art exhibits and hosts many educational programs.

Once we arrive at the visitors' center, we decide first to explore the Bosque trails. From the parking lot, we walk through a small door that leads out to the La Orilla Channel, a cement-lined channel that is now almost dry in the high summer. We walk south along this channel before we find a trail that drops down into the Bosque going east toward the river. To enter the Bosque, we cross a bridge over the Corrales Riverside Drain that moves irrigation water.

This patch of land was part of the 2012 Orilla Channel project that was designed to restore the habitat of the southwestern willow flycatcher, a small bird that had become endangered. This little flycatcher nests in riparian forests and is a voracious eater of insects, so it is important in controlling insect pest populations. It had become endangered in part because invasive plant species were displacing its nesting lands. In particular, the salt cedar, which we have seen throughout the Bosque as an invasive plant, drove out the little flycatcher.

As we walk along the trail, we can see the results of the 2012 restoration project in this region: the salt cedars are gone, and the willows that were planted to serve as the birds' habitat are thriving. Many are as tall as we are in this high summer growth. We didn't see any flycatchers, but we could hear their call from deep in the willows. It's wonderful to see a successful conservation project that preserves one more member of the Bosque community.

Farther along the trail, the willows break open into a clearing, and we see a surprising sight: a young coyote standing, staring at us. It is summer, and this young animal hasn't yet learned that he is supposed to roam secretly through the woods, leaving only footprints to mark his passing. Instead, he looks curiously at us long that we can get a rare picture of this animal that is iconic in New Mexico.

As we walk toward the river, we see many jetty jacks that still march along the edges of the river to keep the floods at bay. These floods are now controlled by ditches and acequias, like the large Orilla Channel that diverts any floodwater, but the jetty jacks remember the years when this was a dangerous floodplain. In other parts of the Bosque, we have seen that the

Young coyote in the Bosque near the Open Space. *Authors' collection.*

jacks are being removed to make firefighting easier, but the removal project hasn't arrived here.

We reach the river that is swollen now because of a lot of recent rainfall and then turn back west to follow the trail. In the next opening in the Bosque, we come upon another piece of public art: the arboreal dome that was erected in 1988, so long ago that the sign describing it is now cracked and worn. The artist was Benjamin Forgey, who has had a long and successful career making organic forms from materials found in nature. This early work of his is a lovely example of his perspective of nature and art. He made this dome using the branches of dead trees from the surrounding Bosque, and he intended it to be a space to where one can sit and contemplate the woods—or for "story-telling, tai chi, or countless other human uses," according to the remnants of the sign.

Arboreal dome sculpture for meditating near the Open Space. *Authors' collection.*

Once more, we're pleasantly surprised at how often elements of art weave themselves into our walks along the acequias into the woods. In addition, so many pieces, like this one, invite the walkers to participate in the art itself.

Just before we come to the Riverside Drain Acequia (that is so important to irrigate this rich area) we are lucky to spot a beautiful bird, a male blue grosbeak. This one is resting on a branch in sight, so we can see his colorful feathers. He sat long enough for us to get a picture. This is a migratory bird, so we are lucky to see him, as he is here only in the spring and summer before he goes south, back to Mexico. The blue grosbeak likes to nest close to the ground in a riparian woodland like the Bosque, and that's just where we saw him.

We cross the Corrales Riverside Drain as we retrace our steps to the cement-lined Orilla Channel. We walk north along it to return back to the small door that leads back into the visitors' center parking lot. From there, we can explore the cultivated areas that form part of the educational mission of the visitors' center.

There is a demonstration garden center that shows the early farming methods early residents practiced in this dry land. While the acequias have served to irrigate the lands for centuries, the demonstration garden shows other techniques the ancients used. In small plots of land, Indigenous people buried ceramic pots filled with water that would slowly release water into the fields. A grape vine grows along the edge of the garden, featuring one of the Spanish contributions to the rich agriculture of the region. As it is midsummer, the gardens are exploding with plants, and the grape arbor is richly green with tiny grapes waiting for the fall to ripen.

As we walk around the back of the building, we see another work of art that captures the community of the Bosque. An old tree was carved with all the animals that live in these woods—everything from a small spider and a snake to the larger iconic animals, like the coyote, beaver and many others. We have to walk around the work and look closely to see all the animals that share our enjoyment of the Bosque. The image on page 80 shows one side of this wonderful, whimsical piece. On the front, it reads "Tree of Life," written in Spanish to capture the multicultural blend of Albuquerque.

The *Tree of Life* looks outward to the lush fields that are managed by the Open Space visitors' center, with the Sandia Mountains in the background. The Open Space visitors' center manages about eighteen acres of land for the benefit of migratory birds and other local wildlife. The farm rotates corn, sorghum, millet and alfalfa. The grains are green and growing abundantly here in the high summer, and by fall, they will be ready for the cranes, geese and other migratory birds to feast on. I'm sure that small rodents, like those carved into the *Tree of Life*, will also enjoy the fall grains.

Tree of Life sculpture in the Open Space Visitors' Center. *Courtesy of Toni Slimp.*

As we continue walking around the back of the visitors' center building, we circle around along a path planted with more native species. Along here, we see several bat houses designed to encourage bats to roost here. Bats are other wonderful animals that live in and around the Bosque. There are actually over twenty different species of bats that either live in or migrate through Albuquerque, and they are essential to the area's insect control. The sign says these bat houses were erected as part of a Boy Scout project, and it is great to see young people involved in maintaining the healthy ecosystem of the region.

As we finish our loop and head back to the car, we stop to notice an irrigation channel that diverts the water from the Corrales Drain into the fields to water the crops. We follow the irrigation ditch toward the sacred space where the pueblo was destroyed, and we think about how the water that moves through these acequias is so precious. It would perhaps have saved the ancient Indigenous people who died under the weight of conquest and thirst.

We arrive at the cars and leave through the Bosque Meadows Road back onto Coors Boulevard, leaving behind this preserved land that embraces its past in its sacred space and the visitors' center's displays. It also looks toward the future, waiting for the migratory birds to arrive and preserving the ecosystems for all the animals (including us) that enjoy the Bosque. It is all tied together by the water that is diverted from the Rio Grande and led through the acequias to make all this possible.

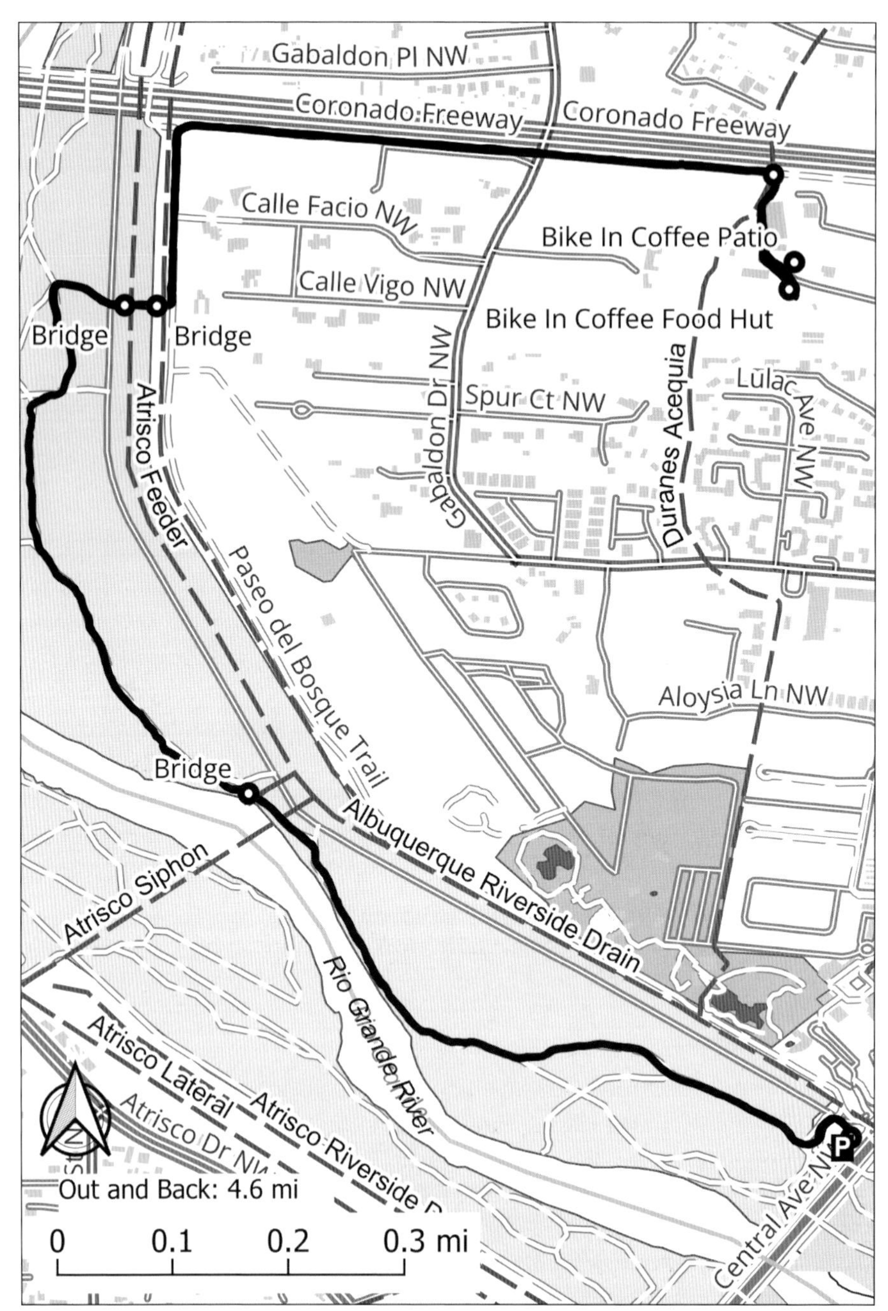

Roger Cardon.

8

MUSIC AND FOOD UNDER THE COTTONWOODS

In 1692, the Spanish colonizers, under the leadership of Diego de Vargas, suppressed the Pueblo revolts that had driven settlers from the Rio Grande valley. With the coming of peace, the Spanish began to recolonize the region. One of Vargas's soldiers, Captain Fernando Durán y Chávez, had been the general's standard bearer, and he brought a petition to Vargas. Durán wanted tracts of land that had been settled a century earlier by his ancestor. This land lay in the valley that is now Albuquerque. Vargas agreed to give him the land. Durán described the land as being "on the Rio Grande, commonly called Atrisco, also of agricultural land with its *acequia madre* and this one in from the bluff where there is an old house… going down to the riverside as far as some corrals."[23]

Durán received his land grant, eighty-two thousand acres on the west side of the Rio Grande. This land became known as the Atrisco Land Grant, and today, it remains one of the oldest land grants in the United States. It is one of the few Spanish colonial grants still owned by the heirs of the original settlers.[24] Durán and his large family and friends settled the land, creating haciendas and raising crops and herds of horses. They also kept large numbers of sheep for wool and meat.

The city of Albuquerque, located in today's Old Town, was founded in 1706, and all the adjacent farms and haciendas, including Durán's, provided abundant crops for the growing town. Of course, this agricultural production depended on water. Durán oversaw the maintenance and expansion of the acequia madre that came with his land grant. This was called the Duranes

Acequia, which weaves north and south along this swath of land as it irrigates fields, gardens and pastures. This is reputedly the oldest registered ditch in North America and is today fondly called the Madre de Duranes. This ancient acequia is shown with all its summer richness.

The productivity of the irrigated land was observed in 1776 by a traveling friar. He wrote of the farms, "They are watered by the said river [Rio Grande] through very wide, deep irrigation ditches, so much so that there are little bridges to cross them. The crops taken from them at harvest time are many, good, and everything sown in them bears fruit."[25] The Duranes Acequia was productive indeed.

This large Duranes community was dramatically changed in the 1960s, when Interstate 40 was built through the area, destroying many fields and homes. The community north of the highway came together to form the Los Duranes neighborhood, which works to preserve the agricultural nature of the old land grant.

In today's walk, we will stay south of Interstate 40 to explore a remnant of the old agricultural land. We will walk to Old Town Farm, which is located on twelve acres of this old land grant. Since 1977, the Old Town Farm has preserved its agricultural heritage. It has served as a working horse farm and grows lots of fresh produce in its fields. This walk is out and back and is a bit longer than our usual routes; it is about four and a half miles long, but we break it up with a rest and a snack in the center, because the Old Town Farm has added a restaurant to serve the bikers and hikers who come along the trails in the Bosque. This is Bike in Coffee, which is open Wednesdays through Sundays from 8:00 a.m. to 2:00 p.m. It serves fresh produce from its gardens and delicious breakfast and lunch fare. This is our destination for today's walk.

We park at a small dirt parking lot next to the river on the north side of Tingley Road. We park under a sculpture of cranes and walk down the adjacent path into the Bosque. We turn north and walk through the cool shade of the cottonwoods. The wild Russian olive trees are high now, as are the willows, all of them reaching their roots down to the river.

As we walk near the river, we soon come to a bridge that crosses water that is rushing into the Rio Grande. This is the outlet of the Atrisco Feeder that finally returns the waters from many of the acequias to the north back into the river. We have walked alongside this feeder from as far north as Sandoval County, and here, we come to its end. This reminds us how efficient the water usage of the acequias is; nothing is wasted, and the unused water returns to the aquifer or the river.

Atrisco feeder drain returning the water to the Rio Grande. *Authors' collection.*

At this point, it is comfortable and familiar to walk in the Bosque with the river flowing on our left. The cottonwoods are in full leaf, so the shade makes it many degrees cooler here than under the summer sun of the high desert. Yet if we are watching, the summer woods offer surprises.

The first unusual thing we see is a great horned owl sleeping in a dead tree, shown in the image on page 86. This owl is native to North America and is widely distributed throughout the continent. It hunts at night and roosts in trees during the day, so you'd think we would see them more often,

Left: Horned owl sleeping in a tree. *Authors' collection.*

Opposite: Bridge crossing the Atrisco feeder. *Authors' collection.*

but they are hard to spot. They are well camouflaged with their spotted feathers that resemble the dotted light in the shade forest, and when they roost, they rest in what ornithologists call the "tall-thin" posture, staying erect and as tall and slim as this big bird can appear. Usually, by roosting in leafy trees, the owl's camouflage works, and we don't see them. Perhaps this owl is less experienced—or sleepier—and chose a bare tree, allowing us to photograph it. We were lucky to spot him, and his position in his tall-thin posture meant he stayed still and didn't move as we took his picture.

We walked on, leaving the owl in peace, but before we knew it, we came across another interesting sight: a white mulberry bush in full fruit. We enjoy eating the ripe fruit as we walk along, and it is delicious. But this white mulberry has a mixed history in the United States. There are many subspecies of mulberries, including those with black and red berries in addition to the white ones. We've seen a number of the bright-colored berries in the Bosque during our walks, and the most common one, the Texas mulberry, is native to Mexico and the Southwest United States. This white species, however, is native to South Asia. In fact, it is the one that silkworms favor, and it was imported many years ago and spread widely. The white mulberry is

considered an invasive species in the United States. In addition to feeding silkworms—and we Bosque walkers—the white mulberry produces large amounts of light pollen, which explains its ready spread. However, the pollen causes many to experience fierce allergies, so some North American cities have banned the plants. We ignore this whole backstory as we happily taste the sweet, ripe fruit.

After walking a bit more than a mile to the north, we turn east to cross two more acequias. Our path crosses both the Atrisco Feeder and the Albuquerque Riverside Drain, and the acequias here are wide, requiring bridges to cross them. We're reminded of the eighteenth-century friar who admired the size of the acequias that required bridges to cross. Some things haven't changed.

We cross both acequias and then we turn north again. Now, we are out of the deep woods and emerge onto the Paseo del Bosque bike trail to continue our walk. This bike trail provides sixteen miles of paved, uninterrupted trails that go through the Rio Grande Valley State Park, and it is an extremely popular ride for bikers. Reviewers on online bike sites call this trail one of the premier bike trails in the Southwest, and its reputation is well deserved. It is one more example of Albuquerque's many recreational features. For us, as we turn north to walk on the bike trail, we just have to remember to watch carefully for the bikers as they fly by us. Many of them have the same destination we do: the Bike in Coffee.

We walk north until we meet the highway I-40. The highway is raised above the walking trail, so we don't confront the traffic, but it still isn't a pleasant part of our walk. This was the road that split the Duranes neighborhood, and as we walk along the edge of the raised road, we can see how intrusive such high-speed roads are to neighborhoods. The walk along here is about a mile long, and the noise of the highway drowns out any birdsong and the sound of rushing water.

However, the highway didn't destroy the entire footprint of the land's previous use. Just before we reach the sign to turn right into the Bike in Coffee, we see water rushing through an opening under the highway. This is the ancient Duranes Acequia that watered the entire agricultural region long before the highway was built.

The Duranes Acequia flows along the western boundary of the Old Town Farm, in which the Bike in Coffee is now located. Once it emerges from under the highway, it is quickly reestablished as the beautiful acequia it always was. The top image on page 103 shows the acequia in its summer height. The water flows high, ready to irrigate the fields, and the summer leaves cause a pattern of shadow as the sun shines on the flowing water.

Shortly after we cross the acequia, we turn right to enter the Bike in Coffee property. Right away, we can see that it is preserving the flavor of the Old Town Farm. There is an old truck with the logo of Old Town Farm that probably dates from the 1940s. It is parked in front of a barn in recollection of the property's history as a horse farm.

We walk past the barn to the fields that extend for acres. There we can see fields that have been planted with produce and greenhouses that grow the early spring crops. The Old Town Farm proudly says it irrigates the crops with the water from the Madre de Duranes. At the same time, they have changed some of the ways the water is used. Instead of opening sluice gates to flood the fields before planting, here, the water is captured in hoses with taps that lead to the fields. These rubber hoses are strung along the rows of crops, and it is a very efficient way to use the scarce water. And it works. The produce is abundant and serves both the Bike in Coffee restaurant and neighboring shops.

After we explore the fields with the surrounding trees, we are ready to relax for a while. We walk up to the restaurant and place our order. Some go for the hearty pozole, the local stew, while others have burritos. Some have coffee or lemonade, and others have fruit and cookies. We all then go to the shady seating area under cottonwoods that are hundreds of years old.

We can enjoy the shade and the food, but there is more. Every day, local musicians play under the cottonwood trees to entertain tired bikers and hikers. It is so relaxing here in the shade, listening to the music. It is hard to leave, but we eventually have to head back.

We retrace our steps back the way we came, relieved to get past the noisy highway and onto the bike trail. Then we drop back into the Bosque, crossing the bridges that brought us here. The mulberry bush is almost picked clean, and the owl still sleeps. Finally, we get back to our cars, tired, relaxed and satisfied by the walk, the food, the music and the company.

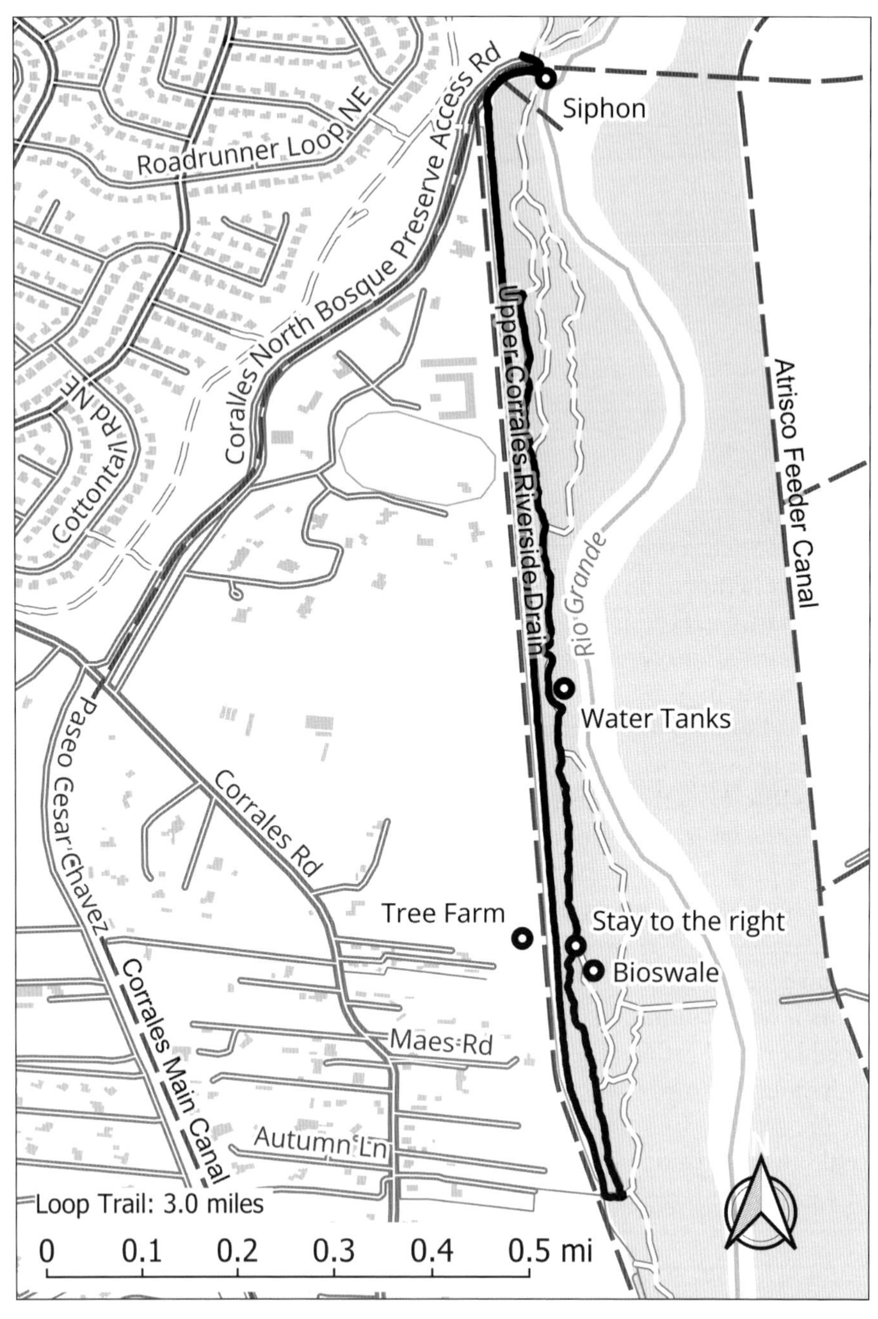

Roger Cardon.

9

FROM FIRES TO A GREEN BIOSWALE

Summer is fire season in the Bosque. The news reports are full of fires that break out in the cottonwood forest, sometimes caused accidentally by lightning strikes and carelessness—and sometimes, they are set on purpose. During our walks in the spring, we saw that forest managers in portions of the Bosque cleared away brush and fallen branches to reduce fire hazards in an ongoing effort to prevent fires. We planned to return to Sandoval County to explore the Bosque trails in Rio Rancho, but we ran into a fire problem.

Rio Rancho is the largest city in Sandoval County, and it is a fast-growing city that is virtually a suburb of Albuquerque. In 1710, this area had been a large part of a land grant to Spanish colonial settlers and was a region devoted to raising sheep, cattle and horses. By the early twentieth century, the land grant had been divided and sold to investors, and it became a boom area for housing after World War II. While its name remembers the years it was dominated by ranches, it has since become a dynamic, growing neighborhood with its own character and services.

Sandoval County is also home to twelve of New Mexico's nineteen pueblos, the homes of sovereign First Nations tribes who were the first to settle in this region. In the last two walks, we have seen evidence of the violence that marked the early interactions between the Spanish and the First Nations. Time passed, and the First Nations peoples and colonizers reached a mutual living arrangement. The Pueblos took what they pleased from the Spanish—sheep and horses and plants and elements of religion—and kept their own culture, based on families, traditions and an appreciation of these ancestral lands. In the twentieth century, the federal government gave the Pueblos sovereign nation status, allowing them to govern themselves. At the end of this walk, we will reach a place where the land shows the modern cooperation among the Pueblos and the other residents of this county.

The river and the adjacent Bosque runs through Sandoval County, so we began this summer walk here in Rio Rancho. We had thought to walk to the Rio Rancho Bosque Preserve, but when we arrived, we learned the trail was closed due to fire. We saw the white smoke rising from the trailhead. As our photo on page 93 shows, the smoke rose behind the fire warning sign that ironically indicated only a "moderate" threat of fire. Someone will have to change the fire sign. Even with the plume of smoke, we could still see the Sandia Mountains in the background, as they are so close here in the north valley. Since the fire stopped our plans, we decided to drive just a short way south to the north of Corrales and start our walk at a lovely spot called Siphon Beach.

In 2020, a rock weir was built across the river here. This small row of rocks blocks the flow of the river a bit to prevent the erosion of the banks. This weir creates a small whitewater flow. We see the beach, with the weir creating the rapids and the Sandias in the background. When the weir was built, a number of kayakers complained that it might be dangerous for the boaters coming down the river. It may be that the weir discourages some from putting their boats in here, but we saw several kayakers launching from this site. They told us they take the river down to Alameda, where they land and go to their waiting cars.

In 2023, the Sandoval Bureau of Reclamation discovered that the weir wasn't enough to stop the bank from eroding. In the summer of 2023, the Rio Grande moved 140 feet, bringing it within 150 feet of the levee that protects the village of Corrales from flooding. Beginning in the fall of 2023, the bureau cleared vegetation from the bank and erected large piles of rocks along the bank. The rocks will remain in place unless they wash into the river, but a long-term project is set to be implemented to shore up the bank line.[26]

We leave the kayakers and fishermen to enjoy this recreational riverbank, and we notice how some of the river water is diverted into the local acequias. Next to the beach is a large pipe with water rushing from the river into the Corrales Siphon Irrigation Channel. From here, it flows south through the acequia along the edge of the Corrales Levee. This pipe is surprising, because the ancient siphons are more subtle. It turns out that this pipe is a 2024 addition, included due to lightning strikes. In April 2024, a lightning

Rio Rancho fire sign with smoke rising behind it. *Authors' collection.*

strike destroyed the electrical pumps at Siphon Beach that moved the water into the Corrales Drain. The original siphon was built in 1933, made of giant wooden planks that stay under the Rio Grande to move the water into the Corrales Acequias. Once the lightning struck, the Middle Rio Grande

Conservancy District officers decided to pump water directly from the river into the Main Canal.[27] This is the pipe we see pumping water.

Unfortunately, every solution brings its own problems, and the U.S. Fish and Wildlife Service became worried about the silvery minnow, that little endangered fish we met while walking the nature center paths. The organization added fish screens on the intake pipes and worked to collect their eggs to move them safely downstream.[28] These fires in the Bosque cause problems that threaten even the fish in the river.

We decide to follow the water for a while as we walk along the levee. The Bosque is to our left, and it is so thick that the river disappears. To our right as we walk, we see ranches and horses, the legacy of this ancient land's use. There are also tree farms, a modern addition to agricultural production. After a bit, we take one of the many trails to our left and drop down into the Bosque to walk in the cool shade of the cottonwoods.

The woods are surprisingly thick here; we are used to walking in the Bosque farther south, where there have been many efforts at clearing the brush and windfall branches to prevent fires. That work hasn't been done here, and it makes a wonderful thick canopy—though it's susceptible to fires.

We soon see one concession to the fire season: there are two portable, inflatable water tanks that are marked with the logo of the Sandoval Fire Department. They have been placed here in case a fire breaks out. The tanks are marked as holding "potable water," so they are for firefighters to drink as they are fighting fires in this area.

Since the fires aren't nearby, we can enjoy the quiet of these thick woods. So many of our walks are near the city, and we often hear traffic noise as we walk. Here, that is absent, so the noise of the woods is readily heard. We don't see them, but we hear lizards scurry away into the brush as we walk by. We can also see in the sand the footprints of the silent coyotes, who are surely watching us from the brush. The predominant sounds here are those of the birds.

We can identify some birdsongs. The mourning doves calling in the distance are easy to recognize. A crow loudly calls before we see him swooping overhead. Scientists have recently noted that crows can count up to four and announce these numbers as they call. Is this crow telling his friends that there are only two of us walking in the woods today? Maybe.

There are other bird calls, but we can't identify them. Suddenly, we get a glimpse of a wonderful all-red bird as he flies out of the shadows. Luckily, we encounter a serious bird watcher, so we ask her to identify this red bird. It's a summer tanager. This wonderful little bird is in the cardinal family,

Emergency pipe pumping water into Corrales Main Canal. *Authors' collection.*

but he is special and hard to spot. The male is all red, which we saw, and the female is yellow-green. We were fortunate to see him, because New Mexico is in his summer breeding range. In the winter, he goes south to Central and South America. We glimpse him as he flits through the trees hunting insects.

Left: Potable water tanks for firefighters to use. *Authors' collection.*

Below: Drone image of the bioswale channels in Sandoval County creating a rich wetland. *Courtesy of Bob Hansen.*

Rio Grande winding along the western edge of Albuquerque. *Authors' collection.*

White porcupine in a tree along the levee near the Hispanic Cultural Center. *Smithsonian's National Zoo and Conservation Biology Institute, www.nationalzoo.si.edu.*

Opposite, top: Drone image of Tingley Beach showing the ponds. *Courtesy of Bob Hansen.*

Opposite, bottom: Piece of a fisherman catching a gar to celebrate Tingley Beach becoming a fishing pond. *Authors' collection.*

Right: Ancient acequia at Hubbell House. *Authors' collection.*

Below: Drone image of the curving acequia of the Shining River. *Courtesy of Bob Hansen.*

Top: A crabapple tree at Shining River, with the Sandia Mountains in the background. *Authors' collection.*

Bottom: Thrush chicks in a nest on the trail behind the nature center. *Authors' collection.*

Top: Globe mallow flowers at the nature center showing another mark of spring. *Authors' collection.*

Bottom: Lady Banks' climbing rose escaping a fence along the Corrales path. *Authors' collection.*

Top: A blossoming cottonwood covering the land with "cotton" along the Corrales path. *Authors' collection.*

Bottom: A blue grosbeak resting in bushes close to the ground in the Open Space near the Riverside Drain acequia. *Authors' collection.*

Top: Duranes's ancient eighteenth-century "Acequia Madre" watering the lands near Old Town. *Authors' collection.*

Bottom: An invasive but flavorful white mulberry bush flourishing in the summer woods. *Authors' collection.*

Left: Siphon Beach in Sandoval County, with the Sandia Mountains in the background. *Authors' collection.*

Below: Bioswale with water running down from the grate. *Authors' collection.*

Right: A startled ostrich along Atrisco Feeder near the Bachicha Orchard. *Authors' collection.*

Below: Indigenous pumpkin at Atrisco Feeder near Bachechi Orchard. *Authors' collection.*

Opposite, top: Bright yellow cottonwoods displaying fall colors. *Authors' collection.*

Opposite, bottom: Bright balloons tapping the Rio Grande in the Bosque. *Authors' collection.*

Right, top: Water rushing along Albuquerque Riverside Drain. *Authors' collection.*

Right, bottom: An example of interactive art: a decorated horse gazes at the Sandia Mountains. *Authors' collection.*

Opposite, top: Soaring cranes arriving in the Poblanos Open Space. *Courtesy of Rinus Baak.*

Opposite, bottom: A large home displaying water in its backyard fountain. *Authors' collection.*

Right: A beautiful acequia flowing behind large homes. *Authors' collection.*

Below: A surprising rubber duck in the backyard of a large home. *Authors' collection.*

Opposite, top: Look carefully to see porcupines sleeping in the winter trees. *Courtesy of Teresa Reinhard.*

Opposite, bottom: Cranes landing in the Rio Grande. *Courtesy of Rinus Baak.*

Left: A carving celebrating firemen's victory over fire in the burn scar. *Authors' collection.*

Below: Goats browsing in the burn scar to restore the Bosque. *Courtesy of Barb Loutrel.*

Top: Acequia water returns to the river in wetlands. *Courtesy of Bob Hansen.*

Bottom: Artwork celebrating acequias displayed near the Hispanic Cultural Center. *Courtesy of Gina Renner.*

After walking for a little over a mile, we climb back up onto the levee as we come to our destination: a green bioswale. The levee drops down a hill into the Harvey Jones Channel. We have been following acequias that bring the water of the Rio Grande to fertilize the lands, but now, we are confronted with a structure that puts stormwater and cleaned sewage water back into the aquifer and the river. This project required as much community involvement as the acequias.

This is a bioswale, that is a green stormwater infrastructure (GSI) that uses plants and soil microbes to clean stormwater and treated wastewater. The Harvey Jones Channel is the only bioswale in Albuquerque that is directly connected to the Rio Grande. It was a multiyear project that reconnected native vegetation in a floodplain with groundwater.

As we follow the sound of rushing water, we come to the start of the bioswale. The treated water from the city of Rio Rancho flows down a grid into a channel. (When we lean over the waterfall, we can smell that this is treated water.) The water then flows down steps and rocks into a pool filled with fish. Then the meandering channel goes north and then east to the Rio Grande through the newly created wetlands. If we follow the narrow path east toward the river, we can catch a glimpse, here and there, of the bioswale channel as it very slowly makes its way to the Rio Grande. The water is green the closer we get to the river, reinforcing the name the Green Water Bioswale. Some of the water seeps into the aquifer, and the rest creates a rich wetland. These resulting wetland channels improve ten acres of riparian habitat for wildlife while releasing an astonishing 4 to 5 million gallons of water each day into the river.

We have a drone photo that shows the bioswale channels as they weave slowly to the river. The drone also captured the kayakers as they paddled down the river!

This project required the cooperation of a number of agencies, from the Middle Rio Grande Conservancy District to the Sandoval County Flood Control, the City of Rio Rancho, the Village of Corrales and others. The group also included the Ancestral Lands Conservation Corps to involve the Pueblos, who also care about the land and the water. These groups gathered volunteers and paid employees to create channels. Crews had to remove dirt and create a wetland area. Then volunteers planted twenty-eight thousand coyote willows, sixty cottonwood trees and hundreds of shrubs and wetland plants.

Here on the banks of the channel, we can see that the land remembers the cooperation among cultures that created this project. The cottonwoods

Willows and cottonwoods growing in the bioswale. *Authors' collection.*

are the native trees, but by adding the willows, there is a recognition of the importance of willows to the Indigenous Pueblo people. As the program coordinator for the Ancestral Lands Conservation Corps said, "Willows are steeped in Indigenous cultures. We use them for prayer sticks during ceremonies and for medicinal purposes. We want future generations to be able to enjoy these cultural benefits too."[29] The willows and the cottonwoods and the other shrubs work together to make this a healthy, natural community.

It is possible to walk along the meandering channels all the way to the Rio Grande, where the slow-moving waters flow into the river. However, it was time for us to return. Since this day wasn't too hot, we decided to walk back to the car along the levee instead of retracing our steps through the Bosque. It is always pleasant to see horses grazing happily in the shade and farmlands stretching into the distance. As we enjoy the peaceful landscape, we are reminded of how fragile these ecosystems are. The Bosque is susceptible to fire, and the acequia needs annual attention to keep flowing. Even the great Rio Grande needs protection from the city's stormwater. The wonderful Green Bioswale project reminds us again that it takes communities, from cities, farms and pueblos to the plants and animals—to maintain this healthy ecosystem that we all enjoy.

PART IV

FALL

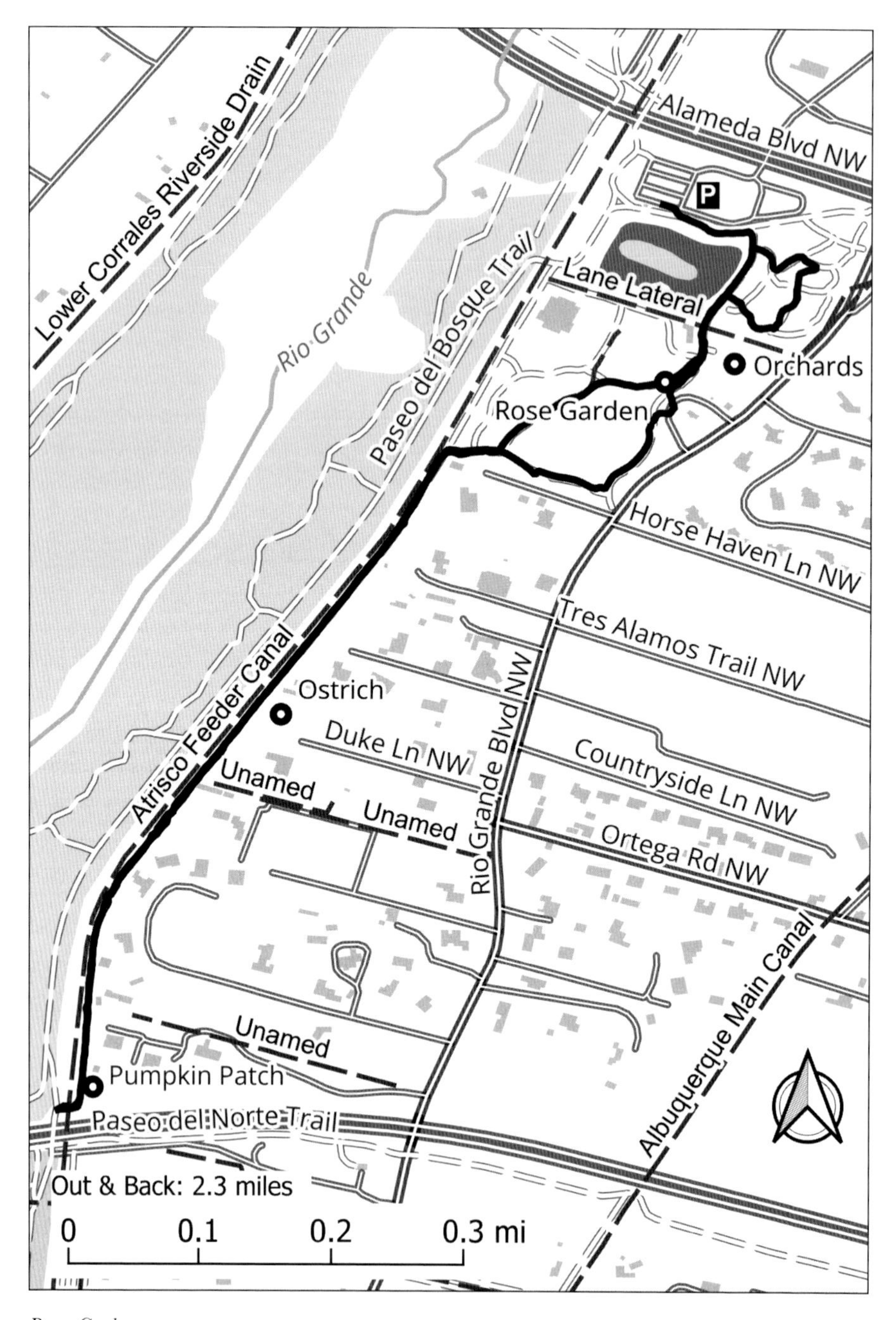

Roger Cardon.

10

EARLY FALL HARVEST AT BACHECHI ORCHARDS

It is early fall in Albuquerque. The sun still shines daily, and only the nights are cool. In the surrounding mountains, the leaves have begun to turn colors, but here in the valley, the Bosque remains mostly green, though the locust trees are yellow and other trees have begun to pale preparing for the fall change.

Here in the valley, this is the season for harvest. The acequia gates have been shut, and the water is returning to the Rio Grande. The crops that have been so carefully irrigated are ready to harvest; the grape vines are heavy, and the corn and sunflowers are turning brown.

Today, we will walk to an ancient orchard that is in full fruit, and this orchard remembers new nineteenth-century immigrants who came to New Mexico from the east.

The nineteenth century brought many changes to New Mexico. A treaty between the United States and Mexico in 1848 ended the Mexican-American War, ceding New Mexico to the United States. In 1850, New Mexico became a territory of the United States, linking its fortunes with that of the United States. (Statehood would wait until 1912, when the Civil War ended the question of which states would be slave states.)

Meanwhile, the United States moved to link the continent with its new territories together in a trade zone. In 1859, the United States chartered the railroad to cross the continent, including stops at Santa Fe. By 1880, the railroad established a branch in Albuquerque, which led to a boom in that city, which was now known as "new town" to distinguish it from the "old town" that had represented the Spanish settlement. The growing new town of Albuquerque drew new settlers who were seeking to make a fortune in the new territory, and this time, they came from the East Coast of the United States, which was seeing its own influx of settlers from Europe.

Two of the new settlers were Italian immigrants, Oreste Bachechi and his wife, Maria. They set up a business in a tent near the new railroad tracks in Albuquerque. Oreste became a liquor dealer, while Maria ran a dry goods store. Like so many enterprising immigrants, the Bachechis were successful.

By 1925, Oreste had fulfilled his dream to build an entertainment venue that would embody the newest architectural principle. He built the KiMo Theater in Albuquerque on Route 66. The KiMo was opened in 1927, and its architecture was unique and remains admired. Maria Orestes wanted the architecture to acknowledge the Indigenous tribes who had been so kind to the Orestes. The resulting architecture is called "Pueblo Deco" and draws visitors today.

However, for our walks, a more important contribution of the Bachechi family is the land they purchased. Owning land was considered the ultimate accomplishment of nineteenth-century immigrants, and the Bachechi family chose a piece of land north of Albuquerque, along an acequia that brings water between the large Atrisco Feeder and the Lane Lateral. This little acequia irrigated wonderful orchards.

Eventually, the family donated the old family farm, with its orchards, to Bernalillo County, which manages a series of Open Space properties. Between 2007 and 2010, the property was redeveloped and enhanced, and this is our destination today. We will see how the land remembers the care of the Bachechi family, as they established orchards that are coming into fruit now in the early fall.

We drive to Alameda Boulevard and then go over the Rio Grande, where we turn right into a large parking lot for the Bachechi Open Space. We walk south to enter the trails. This Open Space covers twenty-seven acres, and we first arrive at the old orchards.

These restored orchards contain their original fruit trees—apple and pear—brought from the north with settlers along the train route. We can admire the remaining ripened fruit on the trees, soon to be picked by harvesters and hungry animals. Most impressive is the large stand of pecan trees that Bachechi planted. The image on page 121 shows this pecan orchard with its impressive trees.

Pecans are the only tree nut that is native to North America. The name is an Algonquin one, and the tree was native to Louisiana, Texas and Mexico.

Pecan orchard at Bachechi Open Space. *Authors' collection.*

When Bachechi brought Pecan trees to plant in his orchard, his neighbors were disdainful, thinking they wouldn't grow. They sure were wrong! The orchards prospered; today, New Mexico has over thirty-seven thousand acres devoted to pecans, and it produces a quarter of the pecans grown in the United States. These wonderful tall trees remember the humble roots of this industry, started by this enterprising immigrant.

Noname acequia between Atrisco Feeder and Lane Lateral empty for fall. *Authors' collection.*

As we cross by the wetlands pond, with its turtles floating gently on the water, we see the Bachechi Environmental Education Building, which was Bernalillo County's first solar-powered building. This building hosts Open Space events and marks the modern future of the space. Yet our view of the building goes across the ancient acequia—one with no name—that created this wonderful agricultural region. The acequia is empty now; the growing season has ended. The image on page 122 shows the dry acequia, with its gate opened and the fall leaves dropping into the ditch. It will remain dry through the winter until the spring cleanup of the ditches prepares for the water to run again.

We continue to walk along the path, and it takes us past vineyards. The leaves are still bright green, though we just missed the harvest of the grapes; we would have seen them heavy on the vines just a week earlier.

We turn to head west toward the Atrisco Feeder that runs parallel to the Rio Grande, and we come to a sign that introduces the Bachechi Memorial Rose Garden. There are still roses on the shrubs, since here in Albuquerque, the roses will continue to bloom until the first hard freeze. The sunny mountain weather keeps many of these plants blooming, even as the fall leaves turn.

Our path takes us to the Atrisco Feeder, where we continue south. Here, we move to private farmland that is irrigated in the spring. The feeder is full, with water rushing back to the Rio Grande from all the acequias up and down the county. The shrubs along the banks are starting to turn yellow as the seasons change. The image on page 124 shows the Atrisco Feeder as it flows along the beside our walkway.

The farms that border the feeder have the usual animals we have previously seen. Chickens wander in their pens, and horses graze in their corrals. A vineyard is heavy with grapes, ready to be picked. The symbols of fall include a small hayfield that has been cut, its grass left to dry before it is brought into the barns, and the ragweed that grows wild—and irritatingly—along the borders.

However, one farm has a surprising animal: an ostrich. While he ran around, he managed to stay still long enough for us to snap a picture. Why keep an ostrich? They are terrible pets because they remain wild things, and they are strong enough to kick and injure a lion, so you want to stay out of their way. Ostriches do lay unfertilized eggs like chickens do, and they are highly prized. One egg can measure over seventeen inches in circumference, and they are equivalent to about twenty-four chicken eggs. Scrambled, they will serve an entire family. Online, ostrich eggs are sold for about thirty

Atrisco Feeder with water returning to the Rio Grande. *Courtesy of Jill Clark.*

dollars each. The shells are also beautiful and sold as decorative items. Is the owner of this ostrich selling its eggs? It's possible. In any case, it's a lovely surprise of come across an ostrich on our walks.

Just before we reach the overpass of Paseo del Norte, we come to a farm that has one more marker of fall: a pumpkin patch. One of the pumpkins is right next to the fence. It's not yet National Pumpkin Day, which is October 26, but this pumpkin seems a nice symbolic end to our walk. We began with the fruits and nuts brought in by immigrants in the nineteenth century, and here, we end with a gourd native to Mexico, one of the original plants of this region. Pumpkins had been cultivated in Mexico since about 6000 BCE, and archaeologists have found pumpkin rinds and seeds throughout the Southwest dating earlier than the Spanish explorations. This simple pumpkin testifies to the agriculture that was here millennia ago, when the Indigenous peoples first irrigated this land.

When we reach Paseo del Norte, we have walked one and a half miles, so we turn around to retrace our steps back to the Bachechi Orchard and our cars. We follow the waters of the Atrisco Feeder back to the rose garden, cross the empty nameless acequia again and return to our cars. Once again, it feels like the land has allowed us to revisit hardworking, prosperous immigrants back to the roots of agriculture here along the waters.

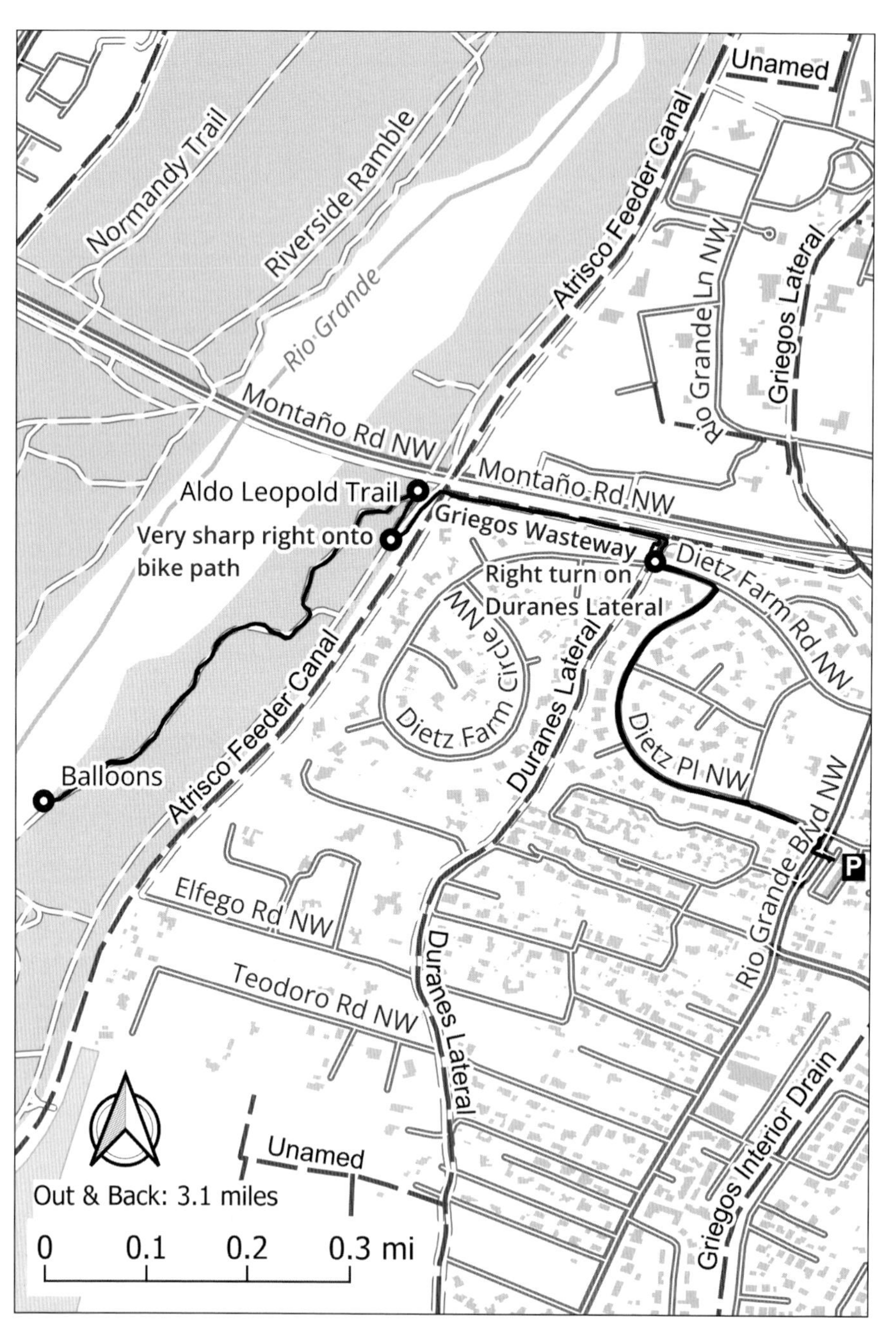

Roger Cardon.

11

BALLOONS IN THE BOSQUE

Fall in Albuquerque is marked by cool nights and early mornings followed by warm, bright sunshiny days. These are perfect conditions for walking—and for flying hot air balloons. Hot air balloons are based on a simple science: hot air is lighter than cool air, so it rises relative to the cool air surrounding it. In 1783, two French brothers used this principle to fly the first hot air balloon by capturing heated air inside a balloon made of silk. The French King Louis XIV was impressed, and a new activity was discovered.

Albuquerque's weather offers a perfect location for flying hot air balloons. Large balloons are filled with hot air heated by propane that flows through a heating coil and lit by a pilot light. The cool air surrounding the balloon is heavy, so the air inside the balloon doesn't have to be too hot to raise the balloon with its light wicker basket that carries the pilot and the delighted passengers. Pilots can make the balloons fly higher with more heat or lower by opening a parachute valve at the top of the balloon to release some of the hot air, cooling it and bringing it lower.

There is no way to steer these balloons; they operate on the whim of the wind. Albuquerque has another advantage for balloonists: a weather phenomenon known as the "Albuquerque Box," a predictable wind pattern that creates a box-like flight pattern for the balloons to follow. At lower levels, the winds come from the north, while at higher levels, the winds come from the south. Pilots can adjust their altitude to determine their direction. This doesn't mean pilots can predict exactly where they will land. Instead, they are followed by a "chase vehicle" towing a trailer. When pilots locate a suitable landing spot, they radio their chase vehicle to meet them. The passengers are then unloaded, and the basket and balloon are loaded into the trailer, all to be returned to their starting point.

As early as July 4, 1882, the first balloon came to Albuquerque. Arthur van Tassel awed watchers as he took off from a coal-gas-filled balloon near the railroad station in New Town and landed in a cornfield near Old Town.[30] Something new had begun in Albuquerque.

While balloonists continued to take advantage of Albuquerque's weather pattern to fly for the next century, things became formalized in 1972. In that year, thirteen balloons were launched in the first Albuquerque International Balloon Fiesta, and it has grown to be the largest balloon event in the world. By 2024, this international event has grown exponentially. Millions of people attend the annual event, and it is estimated that more than 25 million still photographs are taken of the fiesta. This has earned it the title as "the world's most photographed event."[31]

The Balloon Fiesta takes place beginning the first weekend in October. Today, it takes place in late October, but as we gather to walk, we can see balloons rising in the east, framed by the Sandia Mountains. Amateurs are practicing, and tour companies are flying tourists who want to enjoy the sensation of flight and the beautiful, tranquil views. We can often see the balloons rising and descending in unexpected places!

Today, we are walking along the Aldo Leopold Trail, which runs along the east side of the Rio Grande. We met the environmentalist Aldo Leopold in this book's first chapter, as his early twentieth-century work helped clean up the Rio Grande, and this trail remembers his contribution to the environmental protection of Albuquerque. The trail actually begins at the nature center (which we explored in chapter 5) and extends north. As we have already strolled among the nature center trails, we are going to begin in the Los Ranchos neighborhood and catch the northern part of the trail.

We park at the Flying Star restaurant on Rio Grande Boulevard (which is a lovely spot to have brunch when we are back from our walk). From here, we cross Rio Grande Boulevard and turn left on Dietz Place Northwest and left again on Dietz Farm Road. That places us in the Dietz Farm neighborhood, one of the old sections of Lost Ranchos that has been turned into a gracious neighborhood of large houses. By entering the trail this way, we can see another example of how the old rural settlements have been transformed as Albuquerque has grown. This neighborhood has

Spineless cactus in xeriscape. *Courtesy of Jill Clark.*

traditional stucco houses, many behind stucco walls. One of the interesting things to see with these homes is the recognition that they live in the high desert. The yards show an example of xeriscaping, a kind of landscaping that reduces water consumption. This term was first coined in 1981, but now, it has become the gold standard for environmentally friendly landscaping in desert areas. The City of Albuquerque provides funds for people who want to convert their thirsty green lawns to xeriscapes, and this neighborhood offers a beautiful example of what can be done with little water. The image to the left shows a prickly pear cactus that thrives here.

The prickly pear cactus is native to the Americas, and it loves the hot, dry weather. It has beautiful flowers in the spring and fruit in the late summer. The cactus was so immediately popular that it was exported to Europe and beyond, and it thrives in dry areas all over the world.

The problem with prickly pear cacti in the garden is their sharp thorns that can hurt gardeners and children alike. However, there is a species of prickly pear that has no spines. It is called the ellisiana cactus, or a spineless prickly pear. It is perfect for a xeriscape garden; this domesticated, beautiful cactus is popular in this neighborhood. People eat the pad as a vegetable, add the blossoms to salads and eat the fruit directly from the plant. But mostly, it is a beautiful addition to a garden.

As we walk through the neighborhood, we reach a dirt entrance on our right that leads into a trail alongside an unnamed acequia. We turn right to enter the walkway. Since it is fall, this acequia is dry; the gate leading to it has been closed, and the water has been diverted to the drains leading back to the Rio Grande. We follow to a left turn that leads us to the Griegos Wasteway Acequia and cross over the Montaño Paseo del Bosque trail bridge. The bridge takes us over the Atrisco Feeder that sends the water down to the Albuquerque Riverside Drain and then into the river. It gives us an idea of how much water enters these drains from the closed regional acequias.

Then we turn left on Paseo del Norte Trail, a bike path, so we have to watch out for bikes as we walk. Finally, we turn right and drop into the Bosque. After a very sharp right on Paseo del Norte Trail, we turn left on the Aldo Leopold Trail and continue to head south. The Bosque is alive with color, as the cottonwoods have turned golden. The top image on page 106 shows the trail lined with the magnificent trees sporting their fall plumage.

One of the first things we notice (after the glorious color) is the silence of the woods. All the small birds that nested here in the spring and summer have gone south for the winter, and the noisy northern waterbirds, like the cranes and Canadian geese, haven't arrived yet. The silence is fine.

The Aldo Leopold Trail is wide, packed and lacks the thick undergrowth that we have seen elsewhere in the Bosque. This creates a natural xeriscape that allows the desert plants to flourish. The prickly pear cacti flourish here, and these are the wild variety that have plenty of spines. However, we also contend with even more prickly plants. The goat head plants that have a lovely yellow flower in the spring, now have sharp seeds that stick to our clothes (and our dogs' feet) as we walk.

A more pleasant and stunning desert plant that grows along here is the staghorn cholla, shown on page 131. This is one of many plants in the cholla family, and it is native to this region (into Arizona and Northern Mexico). In the spring and summer, it has vivid flowers in shades from red to yellow and everything in between. Here in the fall, it stands sharp in the sun.

As we walk, enjoying the silence of the woods, we suddenly hear a roar coming from the north; it is the various pitches of propane heaters that run the balloons. We see two large balloons descending toward the river. To watch, we take a sharp right turn to the river along a narrow path. On the banks, we can watch the balloons as they lower toward the river, and the propane burners roar loudly; the pilots turn off the propane burners for a silent descent but then turn them on with bursts of sound to slow the drop. The two balloons come down and touch the Rio Grande before they soar up again with noisy propane burners firing. The bottom image on page 106 shows the two balloons we captured as they were descending! They tap the water before they rise rapidly again in a move the pilots call "splash and dash." I'm sure this was one of the highlights for the passengers as the talented pilots showed off their skills. And what a thrill for us to capture this moment!

Staghorn cholla cactus.
Courtesy of Susie Caplan.

After the balloons leave, we notice the river is high. Now that the acequias have returned much of their water to the river, it flows along briskly. The balloons wouldn't have splashed if there were still exposed sand bars, which mark the river in the high summer.

We leave the river and trace our steps back to the cars. As we stroll under the yellow trees, we have to dodge the prickly cacti. All in all, fall is a beautiful time in the Bosque. The colors are bright, the paths are open and the weather is cool.

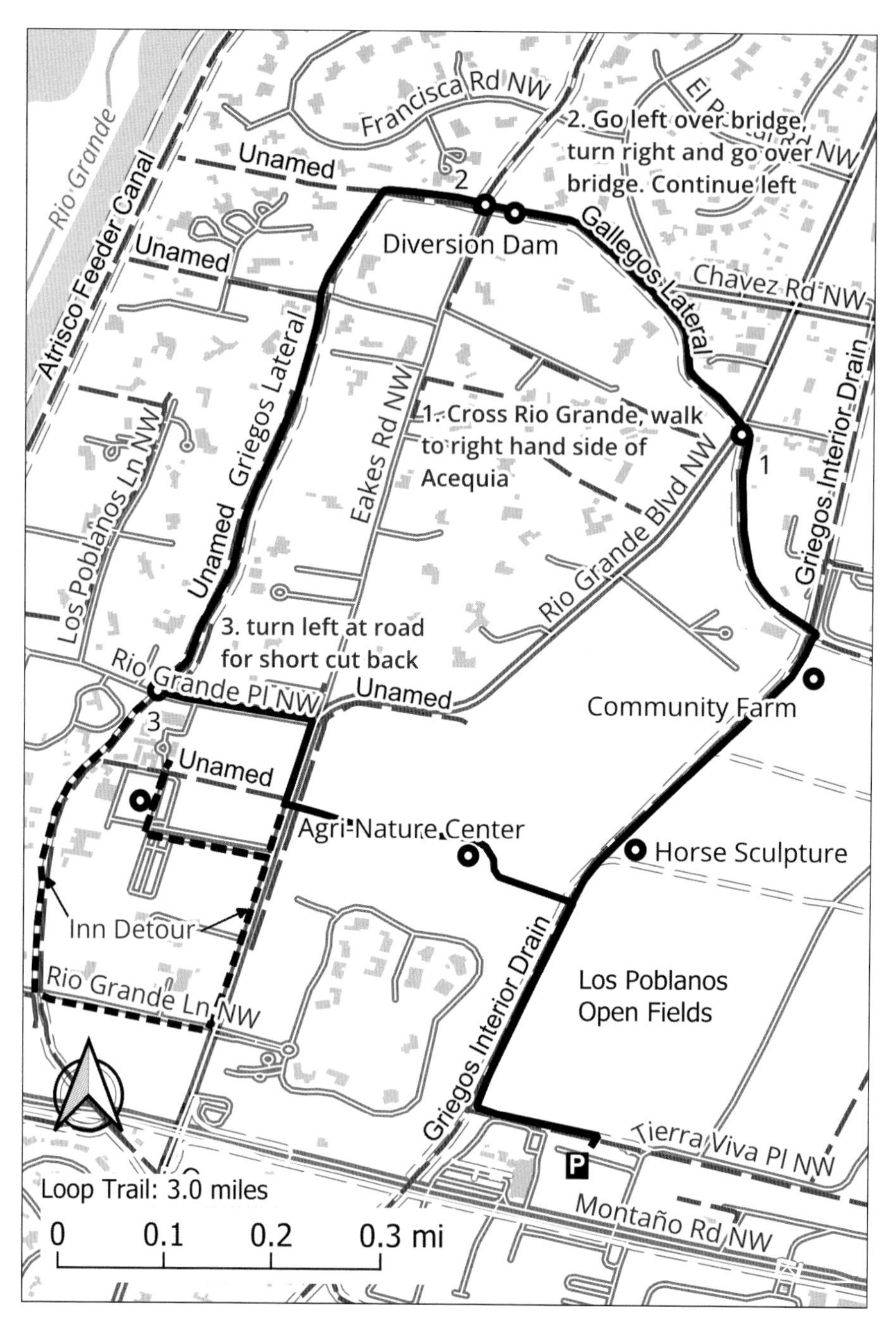

Roger Cardon.

12

THE CRANES COME TO THE OPEN SPACE

The Open Space Division in Albuquerque owns and manages farmlands, as well as Bosque regions. One of these farmlands is the Los Poblanos Fields Open Space, and that is our destination today. This is one of the largest agricultural properties in Albuquerque's North Valley. It consists of 138 acres purchased by the City of Albuquerque in 1997.[32] This farm is one of the earliest Spanish colonial settlements in the Rio Grande valley and consists of a number of fields that are irrigated by the surrounding acequias.

We drive to this Open Space by going east along Montaño Road, turning left on Tierra Viva Road. We enter a gravel lot on the west side of the road to begin our walk, a three-mile loop along the acequias. We cross a small bridge that is over the Hackman Lateral Acequia and turn left to skirt the large open fields of the farmland. A short distance away, we turn right along the Gallegos Interior Drain, a wide acequia that fertilized this rich farmland since the spring.

Now, these ditches are empty, since the water has been diverted. We can tell that, recently, these ditches have been cleaned out by large power shovels. The vehicles have left their tracks on the trail, and the ditches are deep and ready for the spring water flow. Traditionally, the acequia cleanup was done in the spring, when community members gathered to do the work manually, but with the large power shovels, the ditches can be dug deeper in the Fall, secure in the knowledge that they will still be ready in the spring.

As we walk along the Griegos Drain, the stunning views on our right feature the fields, with the mountains in the background. We see several memorial benches along the way that allow people to sit and admire the view. These carved wooden benches were dedicated to loved ones, and most have inscribed sayings about the beauties of the natural spaces. These are worthy memorials in a city where people appreciate the stunning vistas of the preserved natural spaces.

We continue along and see another example of interactive public art. This is a metal horse looking out toward the fields and mountains. Some people decorate the horse's mane and tail periodically to celebrate the seasons; from spring flowers to Christmas ornaments, this work of art celebrates the changing seasons. Today, the horse is decorated with bright fall flowers.

From here, we have a good view of the fields that are managed by the Open Space. Recognizing that wildlife is part of the community here, 25 percent of each farmer's total acreage must be dedicated to crops for wildlife. The remaining acreage may be sold to profit the farmers. For example, this year, farmers are growing oats, sunflowers, and alfalfa. The farms also include sorghum for the wild birds (and other small animals). A flock of wild geese have already landed here to feast on the sorghum.

The last fields are those of the Rio Grande Community Farm. This farm is a nonprofit organization that leases 150-foot rows of urban farmland to people who want to plant crops using sustainable agricultural techniques. The garden provides free irrigation from the surrounding acequias.[33] One of the goals of the garden is to build community, and this recalls the original goal of the ancient acequias themselves: to weave a community together through the water.

One part of the community garden is the Tres Hermanas Farm. This is run by the Lutheran Family Services to provide urban gardening to support families of refugees. Here, new residents of New Mexico can plant culturally relevant produce to feed their families and tie them to the land. It is a wonderful example of one of the urban garden spaces provided in the city.

As we reach the sheds adjacent to the community garden, we see a surprising sight: a roadrunner staying still! On our walks, we have seen several of these native birds running by—they have been clocked running up to twenty miles per hour. This one sat still long enough for us to get a picture, as shown on page 135. This iconic New Mexico bird is stunning.

We reach a gate and turn left to follow the Gallegos Lateral Acequia. The acequia along here is cement-lined, a system that has been shown to be not as good as dirt ditches. The advantage of the cement was that the large

A road runner resting near the community garden. *Courtesy of Carmen Caswell.*

power shovels didn't have to clean it out, but the disadvantage was that the water remaining in the ditch would just have to evaporate instead of seeping back into the aquifer. As we see in the image on page 136, the empty ditch lets us get a good look at the irrigation gates that are opened in the spring to water the fields.

We reach Rio Grande Boulevard and cross it to continue to follow the Gallegos Lateral that ran under the road. As we walk along the ditch for almost a mile, we admire the farms on the right, and the fall foliage that brightens the landscape. We reach a spot where the Griegos Lateral connects with the Gallegos Lateral. Here, a diversion dam has water flowing over it in a small waterfall, as we can see in the image on page 138. The water that had been flowing through the now-dry Gallegos Lateral joins the Griegos Lateral to go back to the Rio Grande. This system of water movement that has existed for hundreds of years continues to work. The water that is borrowed from the river is returned to it again, ready to be borrowed again in the

Dry acequia with the gate closed. *Authors' collection.*

spring. To continue our walk, we have to cross two small bridges back and forth to cross the waterfall of the diversion dam.

Now, as we walk along the ditch, we follow the fast-rushing water. We turn left (south) to continue to follow the Griegos Lateral. This is a beautiful walk with the fall cottonwoods golden in the light, still offering shade to the flowing water. The waterway weaves through the farmlands with horses grazing peacefully (and dogs barking loudly to mark our passage).

We reach another sharp turn, and we go left to continue to follow the Griegos Lateral south for about half a mile, following the water on its way to the river. We can admire the backs of some large houses that enjoy the proximity to the river and the acequias. When we reach Rio Grande Place, we have a choice to make. Some people continue along the acequia to go to the Los Poblanos Historic Inn.

The detour to the inn adds about one mile to the walk. The inn is a lodge and an organic farm that has a wonderful restaurant that serves local food. The inn is what's left of a seventeenth-century farm that was granted to a Hispanic family. As one member of the family said: "We don't consider ourselves owners; we consider ourselves stewards," and part of their stewardship is to grow produce in the traditional way to care for the land and water.[34] There is also a shop at the inn that sells local produce, and a number of walkers stop to buy their famous chili cheese bread.

The rest of us (those walking dogs that are not welcome at the inn) turn left on Rio Grande Lane to continue our three-mile loop. We walk down the road until we reach the main street, Rio Grande Boulevard. We turn south on the road to walk a short way until we see a sign across the street for the "Larry P. Abraham, Los Ranchos Agri-Nature Center." We cross the street and enter the center along a rock driveway.

The Village of Los Ranchos purchased an old twenty-five-acre winery to turn it into the agri-nature center. The property is a center of excellence in regenerative agriculture, which provides organic planting and agricultural education. It hosts farm camps and workshops and does agricultural research. The center is also home to a soil lab and tests new crops.[35] The center was named after Larry P. Abraham, who had been the mayor of Los Ranchos and died in 2018. The center is an Open Space property with free access for walkers and bikers, so we are not trespassing as we enter the property.

We pass by wonderful lavender bushes that are characteristic here. Lavender was originally a Mediterranean crop that was brought to New Mexico with the Spanish settlers. Lavender needs full sun, and the high desert of New Mexico helps it flourish. Tourists and natives alike buy many products made with the local lavender, and the Los Poblanos Inn shop sells lavender products—everything from soap to syrup.

As we cut through the agri-nature center, we suddenly hear a cacophony of birds overhead. The raucous trill can mean only one thing: the migrating sandhill cranes have arrived in Albuquerque and are going to the fields to feast on the sorghum. We can see the flock overhead flying in their characteristic V pattern that served them well during their long migration. As they came to

Diversion waterfall returning water to the Rio Grande. *Authors' collection.*

land, they were so close, we were able to see these magnificent birds clearly, flying to the fields.

The cranes migrate annually from as far north as Alaska, south across Nebraska to wintering grounds in Florida, Utah, Mexico and New Mexico. The migrating birds congregate in what's called a "survival group" as they head south, and they call to each other as they fly. They forage and roost together in groups that may number in the thousands. Their loud calls echo through Albuquerque in the late fall through the winter, and they draw birdwatchers to the Open Spaces and the Rio Grande, where the birds congregate and feed.

Our path through the agri-nature center leads us back to the Griegos Interior Drain, where we started. We turn right on the path that leads past the fields. When we reach the fields, we see that the cranes have arrived before us. They are feeding happily in the sorghum, often loudly quarreling with the Canadian geese who share the bounty. We know it is late fall because of the lavender harvest and—most of all—the arrival of the sandhill cranes that will be here all winter.

PART V
WINTER

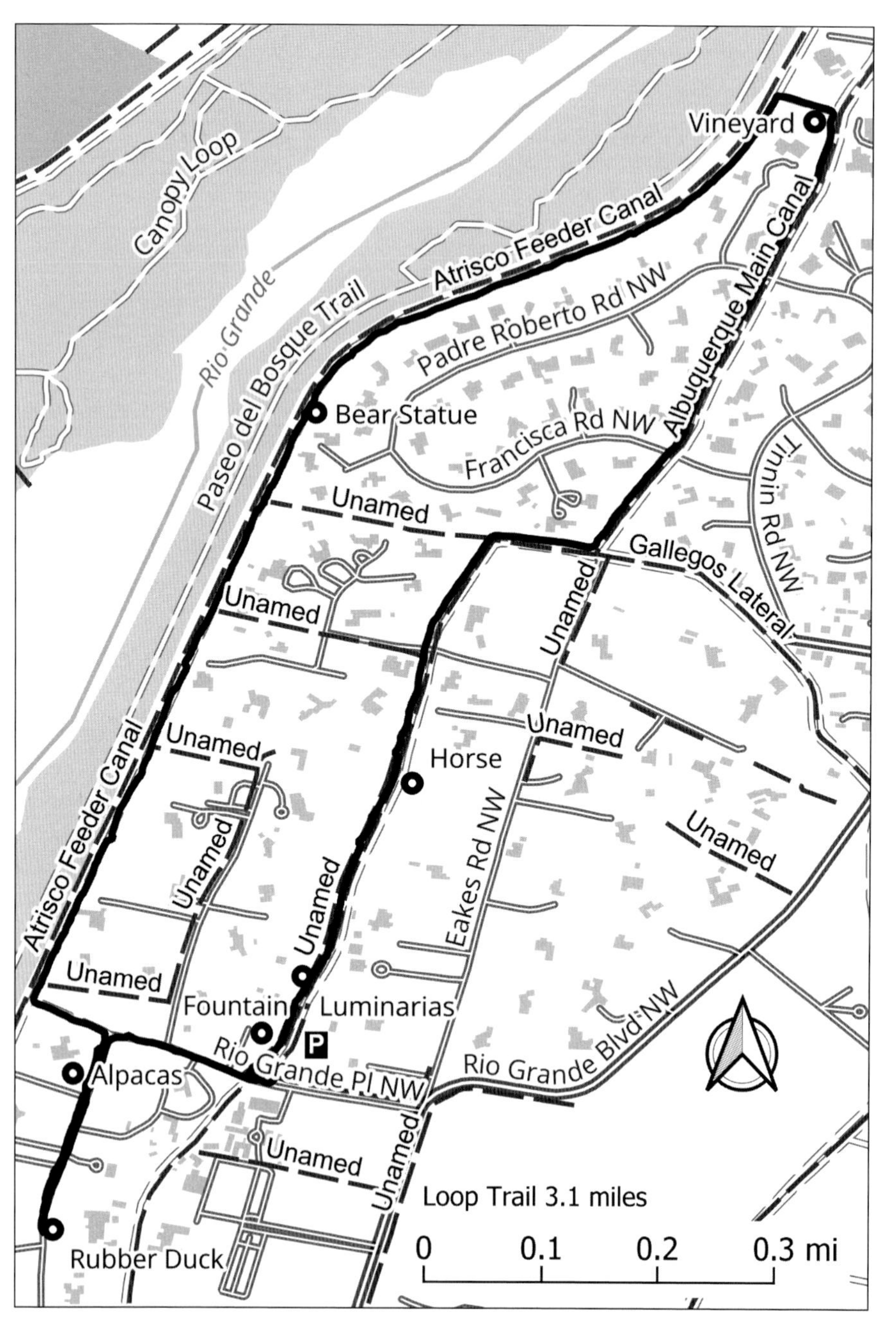

Roger Cardon.

13

WATERING THE FINE HOMES

The acequias mark the spaces of Albuquerque. The Spanish dug the acequias and settled along the living waters as they established farmlands and ranches in the dry, high desert. As Albuquerque grew from a farming community to a bustling city, the settlement pattern grew along the established acequias, even though the new homes weren't using the water to irrigate crops. The map on page 3 shows the stunning complexity of Albuquerque's acequia system. Most of the walks we have taken so far celebrate the farmland, ranches and woods that are watered by the waters of the Rio Grande as it is diverted through the ditches. Today, we will walk along the acequias that weave along a fine neighborhood to explore the urban pattern of some acequias and see the transition from farmland to fine homes.

Our destination is the Village of Los Ranchos, which we first explored in chapter 4. This region of fertile, irrigated land had once been home to Pueblo tribes for centuries. As I described in chapter 4, Los Ranchos was then settled by the Spanish—but not without violence. By the early eighteenth century, settlers in scattered homes along the river came together in various plazas for defense. One of these settlements was the Plaza de Señor San José de los Ranchos, later called the Village of Los Ranchos.

The 1790 census showed that Los Ranchos had about 176 residents living in 40 households. The population continued to grow, and in the mid-nineteenth century, Los Ranchos was the seat of Bernalillo County. However, until the floods of the Rio Grande were controlled, this area remained thinly populated.

In the 1930s, when flood control was instituted, Albuquerque families began to move into the North Valley. In the 1940s, after World War II, a new influx of residents came into Los Ranchos. In 1958, the village was concerned that the City of Albuquerque would annex Los Ranchos, so the villagers voted to incorporate the village. In chapter 4, we explored a rural section of Los Ranchos, but today, we will look at the high-end residences with large lots.

Some of the most desirable homes are built along the Atrisco Feeder Acequia. Even though the residences don't use the acequia waters (those are reserved for agricultural lands), the protected water lands make for a beautiful backyard view. The cottonwood trees are hundreds of years old, and the riparian corridor offers refuge to birds and other animals. Of course, like they are everywhere else in the city, the acequias here are part of the public domain, and we can walk along them and admire the large homes.

To access these acequias, as well as the paths that border the homes, we drive north on Rio Grande Avenue and turn west on Rio Grande Place. There is a small dirt parking area where we leave our cars. This little parking area has an address, 2111 Rio Grande Place, so it is easily found. We park and begin to walk north on the west side of the Griegos Lateral Ditch. Like so many of the fall and winter acequias we have seen, this one is dry, as the photo on page 145 shows. The irrigation gates are visible and closed, and a bridge crosses the acequia to the gates over a dry culvert.

At this time of year, the grass of the farmlands is dry, and the animals eat the hay that was stored in the fall. We can see a shaggy pony with its winter coat nibbling the dry hay, along with cows in the adjacent field. However, the most striking thing we notice is the difference between both sides of the acequia. On the west side, where there are homes instead of farms, things are different.

These homes reveal an abundant use of water. There are expansive green lawns, and one home immediately adjacent to the parking area has an amazing fountain, as shown in the bottom image on page 108. While these homes are located on the acequia, they are not watered by the irrigation ditches; they get their water from Albuquerque's underground aquifer.

Albuquerque is fortunate to have this deep resource of groundwater that has allowed the city to develop, as wells and pumping stations use the water. However, this underground water is not an unlimited resource. We saw in our first walk that the city monitors the aquifer level with many access tubes, and scientists know that changing development shifts this invisible water supply. For example, groundwater used to flow parallel to the Rio

Empty Griegos Lateral ditch. *Authors' collection.*

Grande, but more recently, it has moved away from the river toward the water supply wells in the east and other regions of Albuquerque. Not only has the movement of groundwater shifted, but in some areas, the aquifer is also more than 120 feet below the early measurements in 1970.[36] This kind of aquifer use is unsustainable, and in 2008, Bernalillo County Water Utility Authority began diverting surface water from the Rio Grande to reduce the reliance on groundwater reserves.

What all this means is that eventually, these old homes that used to consider the aquifer an unlimited resource will have to reduce their water usage and shift to a more sustainable xeriscape that can be equally beautiful in a different way. That will come, but for now, we walk along the edge of these large homes and see how they use the water, and some of the most striking features of their water use are the expansive green lawns that are still watered and green in December.

Many of these homes are built in the Santa Fe style, with flat roofs and stucco sides. One home features another New Mexico characteristic: the edges of its roof are decorated with luminaria in honor of the Christmas season. This house is shown on page 147.

Luminaria, traditionally, are fragile lanterns in which candles and sand are placed in paper bags to line rooftops or pathways during the holiday season. Now, instead of candles, people often use small Christmas lights inside the paper bags to achieve the same effect. These are proudly displayed to celebrate not only Christmas but also New Mexico heritage.

We pass the luminaria house and continue to follow this empty ditch for over a mile, enjoying the contrast between the homes and the farmland. We reach a dirt road off to the left (west). Here, there is a vineyard on one side of the ditch with the large homes. This is an example of hobby farms that sometimes appear in this area, where they link the agricultural past with the present.

We turn left at the vineyard and follow the path toward the river, where we connect to the Atrisco Feeder Canal. We turn left (south) to walk along this acequia. The Atrisco Feeder continues to flow with water throughout the winter, which makes this a beautiful walkway that leads behind the large homes that line the acequia.

As the top image on page 109 shows, the flowing water sustains great cottonwoods and provides a home for ducks driven from the dried acequias. The owners of these homes chose well; this is a perfect background for their property. It has flowing water, great trees and public domain lands that prevent any further building. They do have to put up with walkers, like us, who use the public domain walkway, but the path is narrow and overgrown. Casual walkers probably avoid it.

The main feature of this part of the walk, which meanders for a bit over a mile, follows the backyards of these homes, with their expansive lawns watered by the aquifer. The image on page 148 shows one such backyard, with the typical stucco home, green lawn (even in the winter) and great trees.

There are other things to see along here. A small artwork of a carved bear peers through the fence, and a pair of goldendoodle dogs bark at our passing. That's one of the charms of walking along an organic path; there is always something new to see.

Luminaria House. *Authors' collection.*

We reach the first left (east) along the Atrisco Feeder and walk along a road. This is the Rio Grande Place, where we began. However, we are not quite ready to head back to our car. We have one more side stroll to see even larger homes. We take an immediate right along Rio Grande Lane to see more homes, all of which sell for over $2 million.

We pass one low stucco building, a nice, traditional home. This one has two alpacas happily grazing on its rich, irrigated green lawn. Other homes have tennis courts and the more modern pickleball courts. Beyond these

Left: Backyard of a home on Atrisco Feeder. *Authors' collection.*

Opposite: Home on Rio Grande Lane. *Authors' collection.*

homes, we see an even larger home, with an even more expansive lawn, shown on page 149.

This home guards its lands and great trees with a fence.

We could walk along this road all the way to the end, admiring the different homes. However, we stop at one last home that has a surprising feature: a six-foot-tall rubber duck floating on a pond alongside the great home!

The bottom image on page 109 shows this yellow floating duck, complete with eyelashes and a full beak. It is a whimsical reminder of everyone's childhood rubber ducky floating in our bathtubs (and immortalized by a *Sesame Street* song). What is it doing in this multimillion-dollar home? We have no idea, and its presence encourages us to offer equally whimsical hypotheses, none of which are probably correct. However, this duck somehow seems a perfect reminder of the water that has shaped this neighborhood and the acequias that guided Albuquerque's development. Ducks form a nice pair of bookends to today's walk—from the wild ducks enjoying the Atrisco Feeder Canal to the rubber duck captured in the pond of one of the great homes watered by the aquifer.

With such thoughts floating in our minds, we retrace our steps along the Rio Grande Lane to Rio Grande Place, where we turn right. Our cars are in sight in our small parking space, and we complete this three-mile loop from the dry acequias of the farmlands to the green lawns of the large homes.

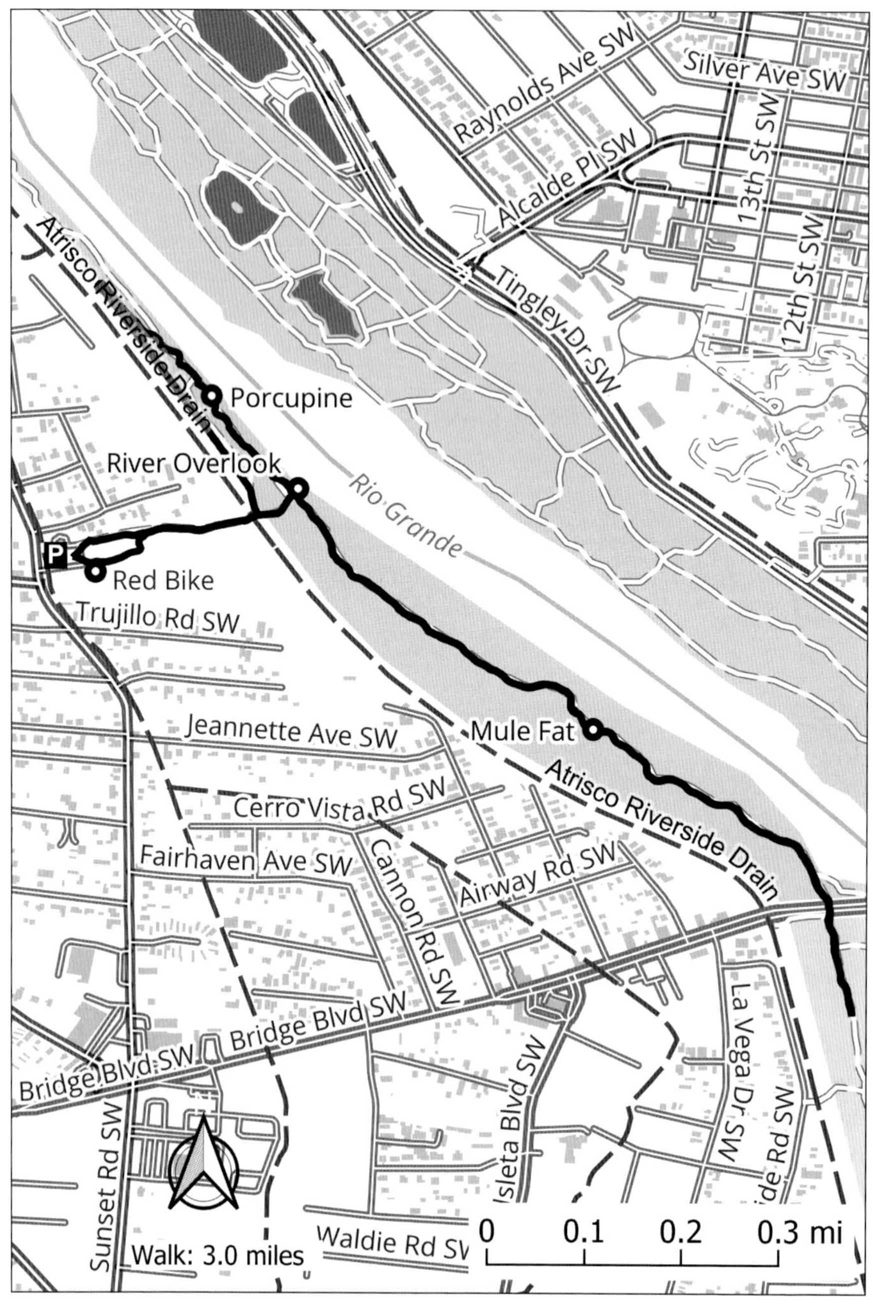

Roger Cardon.

14
WINTER IN THE QUIET WOODS

Many of our walks have taken place on the eastern side of the Rio Grande, exploring the acequias diverting from there. Today, we will go to the west side of the rive to an old neighborhood called Vecinos del Bosque, or "Neighbors of the woods." We drive to Central and Sunset Streets and turn right on Sunset Street. Then we drive south until we reach a park called Valle del Bosque. We turn left into the lot and park our cars.

We've spent so much time walking the acequia and Bosque trails that I haven't written about the many parks and playgrounds maintained by the City of Albuquerque. This city, with a population of just over 558,000, maintains more than 288 parks and playgrounds (in addition to the Open Spaces we've visited on our walks). To show how committed Albuquerque is to its small neighborhood parks, we compared these numbers to some other cities here in the Southwest: Tucson, Arizona, with a similar population, has 132 parks; Phoenix, Arizona, with a population of almost 5 million, has only 185 neighborhood parks. This park is just one more example of Albuquerque's commitment to outdoor recreation.

The Valle del Bosque Park was completed in about 2008, and it contains playgrounds, picnic shelters, volleyball courts and basketball hoops. As we have seen so much public art in the Open Spaces of Albuquerque, we are not surprised to see a large red bicycle work of art set alongside the covered picnic area. The image on page 152 shows this artwork. This piece has a

Richard Rives Memorial Bike art. *Authors' collection.*

plaque that says, "In Memory of Richard Rivas, Community Bike Recycling Program." Richard Rivas was the director of the Albuquerque Community Bike Program, which was founded in 2004. Under Rivas's leadership, the program took old bikes and bike parts, repaired them and recycled them. Then it donated the restored bikes to needy people. By 2010, it had donated over two thousand bikes! This is a worthy charity that combines the best of a sense of community with the awareness of the transformative quality of outdoor activities. This bike memorial is a perfect testament to Albuquerque's community spirit.

We walk past the bike and admire the state-of-the art playground equipment. Of course, all these recreational features were made possible only after engineers made sure the Rio Grande flood control was in place. They restored the acequias to drain the region; the Atrisco Lateral and the Arenal Acequia were cleaned so they could drain properly into the Atrisco Riverside Drain that runs alongside the Rio Grande. In addition, in 2007, members of the community planted more than fifty cottonwood and willow trees to restore the Bosque. These efforts have made the Bosque trails beautiful and attractive for recreational walking.

From the playground, we follow a trail toward the river. We cross a bridge over the Atrisco Riverside Drain. The acequia still has some water in it as it slowly moves south to rejoin the river. The photo on page 154 shows the acequia in its winter state, with the water low and sluggish. The picture was taken facing south, where the sun's rays warm us even in the winter in this high desert.

After we cross the acequia, we walk along a boardwalk to the river, where we reach a nice viewing platform with a bench. On the banks of the Rio Grande, we see a flock of the sandhill cranes that winter here. Actually, a flock of cranes is often called a sedge of cranes. The term *sedge* comes from the marshy habitat that the cranes often like, and we watch as a sedge of cranes enjoy the marshland on the banks of the river.

In chapter 12, we saw the cranes fly to eat the sorghum and other grains that were planted at the open spaces, but these birds are omnivores. Here, on the banks of the river and in the marshlands, cranes can catch amphibians, snails, insects and even small mammals. A group of birds lands to feed, and they call to each other in the river. Their great wingspans of almost five feet show their flying and landing skills. We stop to watch them for a while, noticing their interactions with each other as they feed.

And what of predators? These cranes stay together for company and protection, and when they guard their chicks in the spring, they are fierce. They can kick with their strong legs and stab with their sharp bills. There have been examples of cranes that have pierced through the skulls of coyotes. The coyotes that hunt here in the Bosque will choose easier prey.

Since these cranes have a flexible diet, great flying skills and formidable beaks, it is not surprising that they survive well. In fact, there is a fossil record

Atrisco Riverside Drain. *Authors' collection.*

of sandhill cranes that is 2.5 million years old, making it older than most birds. They are indeed successful descendants of dinosaurs! In these quiet winter woods, theirs is the call that breaks the silence as they call to each other and celebrate their snacks by the river.

After watching the cranes for a while, we decide to turn south to walk along the trails in the Bosque for a while. The brilliant gold of the cottonwoods has faded, though the trees still hold many of their leaves, though they are small and brown. Without the green canopy, the sun shines through and highlights the bark on these old, gnarled trees.

Just as we get away from the trilling cranes, the quiet of the woods is broken again by the raucous calls of a flock of crows. A flock of crows is called a murder, and the loud calls do sound as if they are warning of disaster. Actually, they are calling to each other to alert that we are walking in their woods. We leave them in peace as we continue south along the Bosque trail.

We didn't expect to see flowers in woods in the winter, but once again, we're surprised. The woods are broken up with large bushes that have silvery blossoms of clustered white flowers. The image on page 156 shows one of these large shrubs growing among the cottonwoods. This plant's official name is *Baccharis salicifolia*, and it thrives all over the Southwest. In the spring and summer, bees and butterflies enjoy the plant's nectar as they pollinate the flowers. However, the common name for the plant is much more interesting: it is called "mule fat." Mule fat plants received this name from the days of the Old West, when prospectors and cowboys tied their mules to the shrub. As the mules ate the tasty leaves and blossoms, the animals grew fat (or bloated), giving the plant its name.

The ancient Pueblo people valued this plant as well. They used it to make an eyewash, and the young shoots could be cooked and eaten for medicinal purposes. We enjoy the plant for its beauty, as it breaks up the winter woods.

As we continue south, we notice the rows of jetty jacks along the riverbank. These were the old form of flood control that the engineers used before the river was tamed by dams and acequias. These have been here so long that they are sinking into the bank. In many areas of the Bosque, they have been removed to facilitate fire control, but these are still here and serve as stark reminders of the past, when the river was so dangerous.

Our trail continues under Bridge Boulevard, and we go a bit farther until we've walked about a mile and a quarter. We decide to turn back and retrace our steps. We backtrack until we reach the viewing stand along the Rio Grande, where we began. We decide the day is so nice that we will continue our walk, going north for about half a mile.

The bare trees provide little cover for wildlife, so one of the pleasures of a winter walk is to look for animals that are usually hidden in the canopy. One of our favorite animals to see are porcupines sleeping in the trees. With their

"Mule fat" shrub. *Authors' collection.*

quills, porcupines aren't afraid of many animals, but they do have predators. Coyotes and even horned owls can carefully turn a porcupine over to attack its soft underbelly. Sleeping in a tree is a good protection for the porcupines.

We had seen some porcupines on our first walk, where we discovered they come in various colors, each resting in its own tree. Porcupines are solitary animals, territorial and quick to repel other porcupines who intrude. It is only in the winter that they sometimes nest together, and fall is mating season. The porcupines bear their young between April and June, after a gestation period of seven months, so the females we see in the winter are probably pregnant.

As we walk, looking up in the trees, it is not easy to see the sleeping porcupines. They often look like still bundles high in the tree. In one place, we spot a surprising sight: two porcupines sharing the same tree. The more romantically inclined among us decided this was a mating pair that, together, were waiting for the birth of their single offspring, called a porcupette, that will be born in spring. Or perhaps this was just a convenient tree for a couple of porcupines to nest. Several of the trees have porcupines sleeping; we just have to walk slowly and look closely.

Content with our porcupine sightings, we turn around to start back. We turn right to climb up on the levy to stroll back. This levy was restored by the engineers to control the flooding, and walking along it, we not only get a different view of the woods, but we can also see some of the homes in this neighborhood. We arrive back at the viewing platform to revisit the cranes. Then we return to our cars. We walk through the playground, where children are playing, and we leave, appreciative this community of Vecinos del Bosque, Neighbors of the Woods.

As we walk toward our cars, the quiet of the woods is interrupted again by a sedge of cranes flying overhead to the river, calling to each other loudly as they fly. This is the sound of the winter woods.

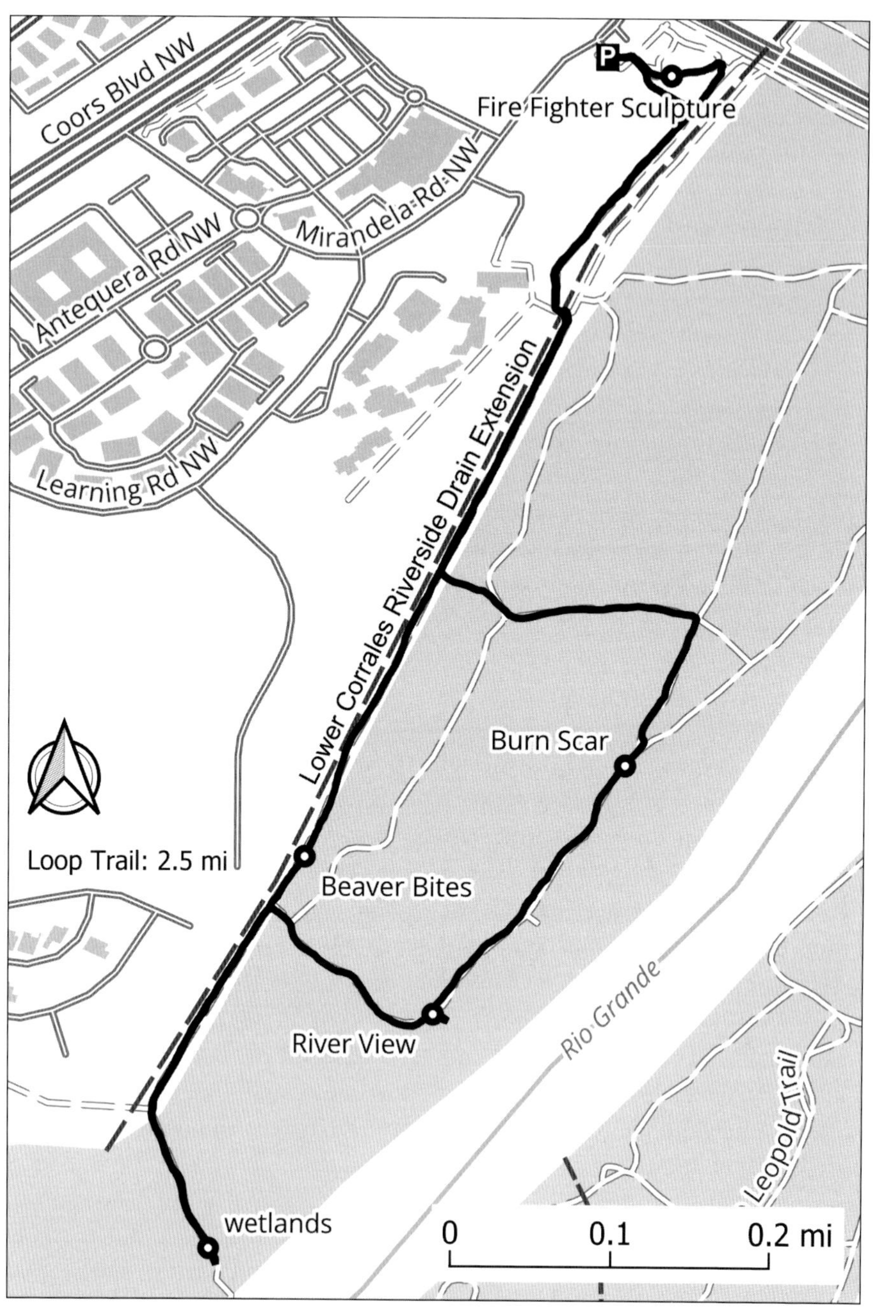

Roger Cardon.

15

RESTORING THE BURN SCAR

Fire is one of the worst hazards for forests, including the great cottonwood forest of the Bosque, and we have seen this continuing concern in our walks. While fires are occasionally started by lightning (like the one in Siphon Beach mentioned in chapter 6), most fires in the Bosque are caused by humans. Sometimes, we drop cigarettes, start campfires or start fires on purpose. Most of the Bosque fires occur between February and early May, spread by spring winds and low humidity.

In June 2003, a cigarette caused a fire to break out near the Montaño bridge. It started on public land and spread to private land, eventually burning 113 acres. After the fire was controlled, the recovery work began. Some of the large, burned trees were cut down and offered to the public as free firewood. Other areas were seeded with native grasses, and new cottonwoods were planted. These tasty small trees were surrounded by cages to protect against hungry beavers that had fled during the fire and then returned.[37] But that was not the end of the restoration of this burn scar.

One of the firefighters, Mark Chavez, happened to be a skilled artist. He looked at the burned trees and saw an opportunity to restore these particular trees to a new life; he turned them into art. He used a chainsaw and chisels to convert over ten trees into beautiful public art. The trees have images that depict the local wildlife of the Bosque. Cranes and eagles peer down majestically from stumps, while beavers peer out of carved holes in the wood. One carving, shown on page 160, weaves together the wildlife and a woman capturing the essence of the community of animals, humans and plants that join together along the waterways.

Carving of a woman with animals. *Authors' collection.*

Chavez's most popular image celebrates the firefighters who constantly guard the Bosque against fires. He has carved a firefighter on top of a tall stump, where he has defeated a dragon that represents the danger of fire. This park is now named the Pueblo Montaño and is the trailhead for today's walk. It was named Pueblo Montaño to remember the ancient Pueblo village that existed here from about 1300 CE. In this way, the park links the past and the present through the art that grew out of the burned trees.

Turning burned trees into art restores a part of the beauty that was lost during the burn, but it's not a long-term solution to the restoration of fires. We can't turn the entire Bosque into works of art. Restoring a burn scar really requires a consideration of the plants and animals of the woods. As we begin our walk at the trailhead of Pueblo Montaño, we can explore the restoration of another, more recent fire.

On May 25, 2022, a police airboat patrolling the Rio Grande spotted a fire in the Bosque near Coors and Montaño. They sounded the alarm, and the Wildland Fire Task Force of the City of Albuquerque set to work. Over one hundred fire-fighters responded; these specially trained personnel set out with all-terrain vehicles equipped with portable drafting pumps and hand tools to begin fighting the fire. Water was pumped from the Rio Grande to try to douse the flames; helicopters were deployed to drop more water. However, this was a particularly difficult fire; the winds were high, and the humidity was low. The wind even helped the fire jump over the Rio Grande and set a fire on the opposite bank, as our drone photo on page 162 shows.

After two days, the fire was contained. Thirty-four acres of the beautiful forest were burned. The bark of the cottonwoods was burned away, leaving dead, white wood; the shrub was burned, and the animals fled. Even two years after the fire, animal counts show that the numbers of animals are still down. For example, fewer porcupines live here; the food the trees provided was burned away. Porcupines had to move elsewhere to get the tender buds, leaves and inner bark of healthy trees.

Fires in the Southwest, in general, are part of the natural order of things. Fires break down plant nutrients and return them to the soil, and some species of plants require fire to reproduce. This pattern is not really followed in the riparian zone, along the riverbanks. These plants, including the cottonwoods, that have evolved along the riverbanks did this to protect the land against flooding. The riparian forest floor stayed moist through repeated flooding; the waters broke down the plant material, and the cottonwoods, willows and native shrubs resprouted from their root systems.

Drone image of the burn scar. *Courtesy of Bob Hansen.*

Over the last couple of centuries, this traditional system has changed. The Rio Grande no longer floods, as we have instituted flood control and diverted waters to the acequias to irrigate regions in the central Rio Grande valley. In addition, nonnative species have found a home in these new conditions of the Bosque.

The most intrusive species, the Russian olive and the salt cedar, love the fires. Salt cedar is particularly invasive and damaging to local species. During a fire, salt cedar burns at a higher temperature than native plants. This heats the soil, making it difficult, if not impossible, for native plants to resprout. After fires, salt cedar groves rebound quickly, further pushing out native species. Furthermore, salt cedar produces high levels of dead leaves and branches that fuel future fires. Any restoration of burn scars includes trying to get rid of salt cedars. Frequently, restorers spray herbicides on the salt cedars to try to control them, but herbicides can spread, causing further damage.

With these considerations in mind, let's start our walk at the Pueblo Montaño trailhead. This walk is about one and a half miles long, but there are enough winding paths in the Bosque to extend it if you'd like. After admiring the sculptures, walk south along the dirt trail next to Montaño Road, and then turn right to walk along the ditch. This waterway is called the Corrales Lower Riverside Drain Extension. It is part of the acequia system that brings the water from the fertilized farmlands of Corrales, and it flows slowly here along the Bosque.

As we walk along the waterway, we see an American coot floating lazily along the shrubs of the banks. The coot is black with a white beak and red eyes. Since this is winter, this is an adult bird. In the spring, we might see it accompanied by juveniles, still grey before they acquire their striking adult color.

As on all our walks, we don't know what animals we will see, but we know they are there. In the woods to the left of the ditch trail, we can see the evidence of beavers. Several trees are chewed; in one tree, a beaver climbed up the cleft to chew on the bark higher up. Our image on page 164 shows the beaver marks on the tree. Was this more tender? I guess you have to be a beaver to know. They dragged some of the branches into the water. Unlike most places along the Rio Grande, where beavers live in the banks, here, the water is moving slowly enough for the beavers to try to build a dam. The rangers who patrol these woods won't let that happen. We can see the dam half broken so the water can continue to flow. Nice try, beavers. They have to go back to the riverbanks.

After about half a mile, we find a path to turn left into the trees, heading away from the ditch to go toward the Rio Grande. The water in the ditch continues its slow path south. Eventually, it goes underground to water a wetlands reclamation region, where the water slowly reenters the Rio Grande. The water separates into many channels as it creates the wetlands that are shown in our drone image on page 104. In this rich ecosystem, other waterbirds and animals welcome the slow-moving water. This image makes a poignant end to our year of walks along the acequias. We've followed the waters along farmlands, gardens, great houses and more, and now, the water is returned to the Rio Grande ,where it began. It really is a wonderful system.

Meanwhile, we've left the ditch and turned east to enter the woods. It rained yesterday, but the earth has dried. However, as we look down as we walk, we can see coyote footprints captured in the clay from the animals' passage through the woods. Occasionally, we can see a coyote in the woods, but not today. However, their footprints testify to their presence.

Our dog started barking at a bush, and when we looked closely, we saw a porcupine camouflaged under some brush. We never see these animals on

A tree with beaver marks. *Authors' collection.*

the ground and wouldn't have seen this one without our dog's diligence. We wisely left him alone and continued on our way.

We then turn right along a trail that parallels the Rio Grande. There are a number of trails that go through the Bosque along the river. It doesn't matter which path you take; they all have interesting things to see! Our goal in this walk, however, is to view the burn scar from the devastating 2022 fire.

We can see the burn from a distance: the dead cottonwoods shine white in the sun. As we approach, we see a surprising sight: a herd of goats browsing in the shrubs. These animals are part of the restoration of the burn scar in the Bosque. The image on page 111 shows the herd of goats busily eating.

The Albuquerque Parks and Recreation Department has contracted with Galloping Goat Grazing service to hire about two hundred goats and a couple of sheep, joined by a hardworking sheep dog named Cue, to browse the Bosque. Goats eat everything. They love invasive woody grasses, especially salt cedar and even the thorny Russian olive trees. It would take volunteers six hours to clear a small patch of land, but goats can clear the same area in just two hours. In most fires, the dried brush would have to be cleared by machines, which disrupt the environment, but goats cause no damage. Furthermore, the goats leave manure as they browse through the bosque. Unlike cow manure, which has to be cured before it's to the soil, goat manure can be applied directly to the soil. The manure has to be pounded in, but the goats handle that, too, as they walk along in the Bosque. The city keeps the goats busy six days a week, replacing volunteers and herbicides as they help restore the burned land.[38] Goats have become part of the community of the Bosque.

We take a side trail to leave the goats to their work as we walk closer to the burned trees. Even two years later, it's still a powerful sight. The dead cottonwoods tower over us, and the salt cedar lines the path. (The goats haven't gotten here yet.) The goats won't eat all the invasive plants; they just keep it at bay.

We continue walking past the fire zone along the edge of the Rio Grande. The water is low, as the river waits for the snow melt in the mountains to flow down and raise it. We can see sand bars in the river, and I wonder at the fire that was able to jump such a wide area as the sparks blew on the wind.

Seeing the burn scar causes me to think about the results of the amazing flood control systems with which we began this book. The salt cedars took advantage of the lack of floods to gain a foothold in the riparian valley. Nothing is simple in environmental change. Now, the community of the Bosque includes firefighters and even hungry goats.

Musing on these thoughts, we find a path that heads back west, and we turn right. We head back to the slow-moving ditch that had escaped the violence of the fire. We meander along its banks, seeing the coot still floating along as we head back to Pueblo Montaño.

Conclusion

WATER IS NOT A COMMODITY

Kim has been guiding groups through these trails for years, exploring every nook and cranny of the acequia trails. When Joyce joined the group, she recognized the acequias were similar to the age-old water systems in Spain. Now, we've completed a year's worth of walks, exploring the wonderful trails that offer different sights in every season. We have learned that the land remembers its history, as plants and animals testify to the original inhabitants and the coming of new peoples through the region. We saw how the layout of the city wove around the ancient acequias that moved water from the river through the communities. And as we have seen throughout this book, walking in nature encouraged all kinds of conversations, but at the end of the day, walking the acequias came down to water. Our conversations inevitably strayed to the larger, ongoing questions of how to handle water in an age of climate change and increasing water scarcity.

The question of how to use precious water isn't unique to New Mexico. A wonderful collection of essays, called *Water for the People*, published in 2023, shows the how acequia cultures have sustained communities all over the world from New Mexico and Spain to Chile, Yemen and beyond.[39] Our small microhistory of two New Mexico counties' acequias fits into a global analysis of how people use water to sustain life. How should we think about water?

When we pay our water bill, we are encouraged to think about water as a commodity that we have purchased. Historically, water has been connected to a piece of land; people have fought over the water in a well on their land. In 1907, a Water Code was passed in New Mexico that separated land from water and made water a commodity that could be purchased and, indeed, sold.[40] Even the great rivers, like the Colorado, are the subject of dispute among the states that use the water. People in the upper Midwest have engaged in discussions about whether the water in their Great Lakes is for sale.[41] The consensus is, no—the water is not for sale. The members of the New Mexico Acequia Association say: "El agua no se vende, el agua se defiende." "Water is not for sale, water is to be defended."[42] So, if water isn't a commodity, what is it?

A wonderful new novel by Elif Shafak traces the same drop of water from antiquity to modern times.[43] It reminds us that no water is lost. All our planetary water has been with us as long as the Earth; it is just moved around. Shafak invites us to think of water not as commodity but as a companion, joining us in our own journey. This vision comes closer to the acequia ideal in its recognition that water is not a commodity, but it doesn't argue for its defense.

The acequia culture suggests that water is part of the community and should be treasured and treated as such. This is what we noticed as we began to walk the acequia trails: a community is woven together and supported by the running of the waters. The paths tie together plants, animals, and neighborhoods in a historical relationship that endures today.

The waters' flow reinforces the idea that it is borrowed, not bought. The waters move into the irrigation ditches, water the plants and then move back into the ditches before returning to the river. Water seeps into the aquifer as it moves along, contributing to the communities' water supply.

We were also pleasantly surprised to see how the land remembers the layers of people, plants and animals that have settled here, fed by the ancient water systems. As this book details, we saw remnants of the Indigenous tribes, and we saw the plants and animals the Spanish brought. We followed the modern additions to the acequia community, with everything from alpacas to solar panels. The community that is nurtured by the waters is complex and embraces the past and the present, all sustained by the acequias. What also became pleasantly evident is that our walking group, too, became part of this community of water.

In 2024, an award-winning filmmaker, Arcie Chapa, made a documentary called *Acequias: The Legacy Lives On*, which won the Best Documentary Award at the 2024 Santa Fe Film Festival. It has been shown on PBS to much acclaim. This documentary brings the history of the acequias from its past to its immediately relevant present with interviews with farmers, scholars, and members of the community. The poignant testimonials, combined with visually stunning images, reveal how important the acequias continue to be today, and they show how the acequias aren't simply irrigation ditches but also a community that draws people together. The film refers not simply to "acequias" but "acequia communities." This is what the water is, a "culturally green" phenomenon that preserves not only the scare water but also the culture that depends on it. As a matter of fact, Chapa concludes that the acequias are the single most important infrastructure in New Mexico. This may be, though we might vote for electricity as a top infrastructure, but Chapa's designation reveals the importance of these ditches. However, in addition to the acequias' existential value, we discovered the acequia trails also offer a pleasurable walk into nature, the past and the vibrant present.

We started our acequia walking project when New Mexico celebrated the acequias with a license plate. As we finished our journeys, Albuquerque celebrated the acequias in a characteristic New Mexico fashion: through art. The Art in Public Places project joined with the National Hispanic Cultural Center to create a project to called the Acequia Revitalization Project. The project is as ambitious as the flowing water itself. It was intended to "explore the following ideas: acequias, water, movement, journeys, voyages, passageways, connections, the river, the history of acequias, and water al life."[44]

The artist Reyes Padilla worked with youth to make a mosaic mural on the acequia project. The artist celebrated the project saying, "Acequias are like magic."[45] We decided to take one final short walk to the Hispanic Cultural Center to see this work of art. The art is a 260-foot-long concrete piece that winds like a river on the southern side of the building. Along one side, there is a mosaic river that extends along the 520 feet of the surface. The mosaic river winds among silhouettes of significant features of the acequia; we see people clearing the ditches and the mayordomo overseeing the cleaning. Then the images show the results of the harvest: corn, chiles and other crops. On the other side of the winding concrete structure, the artist has portrayed more crops that make up the richness of an irrigated New Mexico.

As we were admiring and taking pictures of the artwork, we stopped to talk to a man who was tinkering with the tiles on the mosaic. It was the artist, Reyes Padilla! Sometimes, encounters on our walks are totally serendipitous—a coyote, a balloon or an artist! Padilla was kind enough to talk to us about his vision of this art that has taken a couple of years to bring to fruition. He told us how pleased he is to show how the acequias are important to New Mexico and how they are central to the communities that share and care for the water. And he showed us the best place to take a picture to capture this large piece of art. We took his advice and captured the mosaic side and mural side, framed by the flags of South America that celebrate the Hispanic heritage of New Mexico.

This artwork vividly demonstrates that the water in the acequias is so much more than a commodity that we purchase. It is indeed the lifeblood that creates a rich community. As we close this literary journey along the vital acequias, we come away grateful for the waters that have nourished the land, its life and our community of walkers. We have been enriched by our walks and hope that you have also enjoyed the journey, whether you walk or simply read about these rich community trails.

NOTES

Introduction

1. Lamadrid and Rivera, *Water for the People*, 6–7.
2. "USACE Acequia Rehabilitation and Restoration Program," U.S. Army Corps of Engineers, https://www.spa.usace.army.mil/Missions/Civil-Works/Acequia-Program/.
3. Audrey Claire Davis, "New Mexico Unveils New Specialty Acequia License Plate," KRQE, December 20, 2023, https://www.krqe.com/news/new-mexico/new-mexico-unveils-new-specialty-acequia-license-plate/.
4. Rodríguez, *Acequia*, 81–82.
5. Feliz Romero, "Acequia Celebration and Fun Run Raises Awareness on the Importance of Water," KOB, April 14, 2024, https://www.kob.com/new-mexico/acequia-celebration-and-fun-run-raises-awareness-about-the-importance-of-water/?utm_source=ground.news&utm_medium=referral.
6. Jay Maddock, director of the Center for Health and Nature, Texas A&M, interview, July 4, 2024. See, www.naturequant.com.
7. Williams, *Nature Fix*, n.p.
8. "Copyright and License," OpenStreetMap, https://www.openstreetmap.org/copyright.

Chapter 1

9. Yasmeen Najmi, "Conservation in the Conservancy District," in *Water for the People*, 88.
10. Schmader, *Albuquerque's Parks*, 34.

Chapter 2

11. Schmader, *Albuquerque's Parks*, 53.

Chapter 3

12. Rivera, *Acequia Culture*, 3.
13. Rivera, *Acequia Culture*, 15.
14. Rivera, *Acequia Culture*, 10.

Chapter 4

15. Carol J. Condie, ed., "Los Ranchos Plaza (LA46638): Test Excavations at a Spanish Colonial Settlement in Bernalillo County, New Mexico, 1996–1997," Maxwell Museum Technical Series No. 4 (Maxwell Museum of Anthropology, University of New Mexico, 2007), 13–24.
16. "39. Bosque Songs," The Bosque Education Guide, New Mexico Museum of Natural History and Science, https://nmnaturalhistory.org/sites/default/files/documents/education/BosqueEdGuide/Chapter5_39_BosqueSongs.pdf.

Chapter 5

17. "Burque Bee City USA," City of Albuquerque, https://www.cabq.gov/parksandrecreation/open-space/bee-city-usa.
18. "Rio Grande Silvery Minnow," U.S. Fish and Wildlife Service, https://www.fws.gov/species/rio-grande-silvery-minnow-hybognathus-amarus.
19. World-Wide Labyrinth Locator, https://labyrinthlocator.com/.

Chapter 6

20. Kate Ashford, Andrea Bartz, Jeff Cox, Asa Fitch, Stephen Gandel, Josh Hyatt, Rob Kelley, Kathleen Knight, et al., "Best Places to Live: Top 100," CNN Money, 2007, https://money.cnn.com/galleries/2007/moneymag/0707/gallery.BPTL_top_100.moneymag/19.html.

Chapter 7

21. Matt Schmader, "Thundersticks and Coats of Iran: Recent Discoveries at Piedras Marcadas Pueblo, New Mexico," in Flint and Flint, *Latest Word from 1540*, 308–47.
22. "Open Space Visitor Center," City of Albuquerque, https://www.cabq.gov/parksandrecreation/open-space/open-space-visitor-center.

Chapter 8

23. Sanchez, *Don Fernando Durán*, 9–10.
24. "Petroglyph: History of the Atrisco," National Park Service, https://www.nps.gov/petr/learn/historyculture/atrisco.htm.
25. Domínguez, *Missions of New Mexico*, 151.

Chapter 9

26. Cathy Cook, "Siphon Beach Temporarily Closed to Address Erosion in the Bosque," *Albuquerque Journal*, November 20, 2023.
27. Theresa Davis, "Emergency Pumps and Pipes Installed to Serve Corrales Irrigators," *Albuquerque Journal*, April 21, 2022, https://www.abqjournal.com/news/local/article_c558731b-2936-5680-8ca9-fdfcdedd0e6c.html.
28. Davis, "Pumps and Pipes Installed."
29. Tracey Stone, "A Recreational Gem, 15 Minutes from Urban Area, Offers Beauty, Calm," The Nature Conservancy, January 21, 2024, https://www.nature.org/en-us/newsroom/new-mexico-harvey-jones-walk/.

Chapter 11

30. Schmader, *Albuquerque's Parks*, 18.
31. "History," Albuquerque International Balloon Festival, https://balloonfiesta.com/History.

Chapter 12

32. "Open Space Farmlands," City of Albuquerque, https://www.cabq.gov/parksandrecreation/open-space/lands/open-space-farmlands.
33. Rio Grande Community Farm, https://riograndefarm.org/.
34. Gwyneth Doland, "Los Ranchos de Albuquerque Is Rooted in the River," *New Mexico Magazine*, July 28, 2021, https://www.newmexicomagazine.org/blog/post/los-ranchos-de-albuquerque-rooted-in-the-river.
35. "Welcome to the Larry P. Abraham Agri-Nature Center and Agriculture Program," The Village of Los Ranchos de Albuquerque, https://www.losranchosnm.gov/agcenter.

Chapter 13

36. Steven Rice, Gretchen Oelsner and Charles Heywood, "Simulated and Measured Water Levels and Estimated Water-Level Changes in the Albuquerque Area, Central New Mexico, 1950–2012," Scientific Investigations Map 3305, U.S. Geological Survey, July 16, 2014, https://pubs.usgs.gov/sim/3305/.

Chapter 15

37. "Chapter 6: Fire in the Rio Grande Bosque," The Bosque Education Guide, New Mexico Museum of Natural History and Science, https://nmnaturalhistory.org/bosque-education-guide/chapter-6-fire-rio-grande-bosque.
38. "No Kidding: How Goats are Helping the Bosque Recover After Fire," *Albuquerque Journal*, January 29, 2024.

Conclusion

39. Lamadrid and Rivera, *Water for the People*, n.p.
40. Lamadrid and Rivera, *Water for the People*, xvii.
41. Dempsey, *Great Lakes for Sale*, n.p.
42. Lamadrid and Rivera, *Water for the People*, xvii.
43. Shafak, *Rivers in the Sky*, n.p.
44. Adrian Gomez, "Aquatic Journey: The Acequia Revitalization Project Explores Water Movement Through Mosaic Art," *Albuquerque Journal*, September 1, 2024, https://www.abqjournal.com/lifestyle/aquatic-journey-the-acequia-revitalization-project-explores-water-movement-through-mosaic-art/article_fde5c0ec-65b3-11ef-a6d8-9f118473f925.html.
45. Gomez, "Aquatic Journey."

SELECTED BIBLIOGRAPHY

Bannerman, Ty. *Forgotten Albuquerque*. Arcadia Publishing, 2009.

Clark, Ira G. *Water in New Mexico: A History of Its Management and Use*. University of New Mexico Press, 1987.

Crawford, Stanley. *Mayordomo: Chronicle of an Acequia in Northern New Mexico*. University of New Mexico Press, 1988.

Dempsey, Dave. *Great Lakes for Sale*. Updated edition. Mission Point Press, 2021.

Domínguez, Francisco Atanasio. *The Missions of New Mexico, 1776*. Sunstone Press, 2012.

Flint, Richard, and Shirley Cushing Flint, eds. *The Latest Word from 1540: People, Places and Portrayals of the Coronado Expedition*. University of New Mexico Press, 2011.

Glick, Thomas F. *Irrigation and Society in Medieval Valencia*. Belknap Press of Harvard University Press, 1970.

LaFarge, Oliver. *The Mother Ditch: La Acequia Madre*. Sunstone Press, 1983.

Lamadrid, Enrique R., and José Rivera, eds. *Water for the People: The Acequia Heritage of New Mexico in a Global Context*. University of New Mexico Press, 2023.

Meyer, Michael C. *Water in the Hispanic Southwest*. University of Arizona Press, 1984.

Palmer, Mo. *Albuquerque Then and Now*. Pavilion Books, 2019.

Price, V.B. *Albuquerque: City at the End of the World*. 2nd ed. University of New Mexico Press, 2003.

Rivera, José. *Acequia Culture: Water, Land, and Community in the Southwest*. University of New Mexico Press, 1998.

Rodríguez, Sylvia. *Acequia: Water Sharing, Sanctity, and Place*. School for Advanced Research, 2006.

Sanchez, Joseph P. *Don Fernando Durán y Chaves's Land and Legacy*. National Park Service, 1998.

Sargeant, Kathryn, and Mary P. Davis. *Shining River, Precious Land: An Oral History of Albuquerque's North Valley*. Albuquerque Museum, 1995.

Schmader, Matt. *Albuquerque's Parks and Open Space*. Arcadia Publishing, 2011.

Shafak, Elif. *There Are Rivers in the Sky*. Random House, 2024.

Williams, Florence. *The Nature Fix: Why Nature Makes Us Happier, Healthier, and More Creative*. W.W. Norton & Company, 2017.

ABOUT THE AUTHORS

Courtesy of Lupe García.

Joyce Salisbury is a medieval historian who has written more than ten books, including, most recently, *The First Christian Communities, 32–380 CE* (Routledge, 2024). She has also written and recorded four streaming series for Great Courses, including, most recently, *The Mediterranean World*. Salisbury has also appeared on the history channel and PBS and remains in demand as a lecturer. Much of Salisbury's work weaves history and geography, and this book reflects that interest. When she moved to New Mexico, Salisbury recognized the Spanish irrigation ditches that resembled those in Spain, so she was excited to study this ancient water use that remains vibrant and important in New Mexico.

Kim Hafermalz is an experienced and skilled trail guide. She has volunteered with Albuquerque Open Space as part of their trails team and explored and wandered the many trails throughout the Bosque (the cottonwood forest along the Rio Grande River). She has also led a twice-weekly walking group that she organized. Over many years, she has drawn on her extensive knowledge of the Open Space trails, local guidebooks, other walkers and Google Earth to expand the number of season-appropriate walks that have been organized in this book.